Jean Renart

*THE LAI DE L'OMBRE*

Jean Renart

*THE LAI DE L'OMBRE*


Edited from manuscript E
[B. N. *nouv. acq. fr.* 1104]


by

Margaret E. Winters

Summa Publications, Inc.
Birmingham, Alabama
1986

Copyright 1986
Summa Publications, Inc.

ISBN 0-917786-40-8

Library of Congress Catalog Card Number  86-60800

Printed in the United States of America

To my parents, Dorothy and Joseph Winters,

with love

# TABLE OF CONTENTS

# Preface

This new edition of Jean Renart's *Lai de l'ombre* was prepared for two reasons: first of all, no critical edition has ever been done of the version found in ms. *E*, a manuscript which, if not superior to *A*, is certainly its equal. And the poem itself merits more attention in the classroom: it is relatively short, written in a dialect which is not heavily marked by regionalisms, and, perhaps more important, it is fun to read. The apparatus, therefore, was prepared to serve the double purpose of providing a study of ms. *E* and its version of the poem for the Old French specialist, and also a text which might aid the novice in learning to read this language and appreciate its literature. The notes and glossary, accordingly, are fuller than they might otherwise have been.

I would like to acknowledge the Grant-in-Aid from the American Philosophical Society, which enabled me to work in Paris at the Bibliothèque Nationale, and the help of the University of Pennsylvania Microfilm Project from which I obtained microfilms and the necessary printed photocopies to work on text and variants.

To several individuals go gratitude and affection for their help with "my" *Lai*: to William Roach of the University of Pennsylvania for reading and commenting on sections of the edition; to Linda Ober, who typed, and Dorothy Stegman, Michael Anders, Stefan Fodor, Dorothy Winters, and Geoffrey Nathan, who helped proofread, all with patience and humor as well as great care; to Geoffrey Nathan, who has encouraged me to keep going; and finallly to the students in my various History of French courses at the University of Pennsylvania and Southern Illinois University who provided questions, objections, and varied reactions to versions of the text and glossary over the last few years. *Vobis omnibus gratias sinceras ago!*

# INTRODUCTION

## Manuscripts and Editions

*Manuscripts and their Filiation*

There are seven manuscript versions of the *Lai de l'ombre*, all in Paris, at the Bibliothèque Nationale. The sigla below have been in use since Bédier's 1890 edition:[1]

A = *f. fr.* 837, f. 40r-44v; collection of verse *fabliaux* and tales; 13th century.

B = *f. fr.* 1593, f. 157r-162v; various songs, etc.; 13th century.

C = *f. fr.* 12603, f. 249v-255r; collection of Old French poetry including the *Chevalier as deus espees*, the *Chevalier au Lion, Enfances Ogier, Fierabras*, lays, fables, and fragments of *Brut, Eneas*; 13th-14th century.

D = *f. fr.* 19152, f. 85v-89r; collection of *fabliaux*, tales, fables, proverbs, including *Partonopeus de Blois, Blancandrin*; 13th century.

E = *nouv. acq. fr.* 1104, f. 54v-61r; collection of Breton lays; 13th century. See description, pp.

F = *f. fr.* 14971, f. 48v-56v; fables of Marie de France; 14th century.

G$^2$ = *f. fr.* 1553, f. 493v-498r; mixed collection including the *Roman de Troyes, Roman de la Violette, Eustasse le moine*; 13th century.

The manuscript filiation of the *Lai de l'ombre* is perhaps the most thoroughly studied one in the literature, since it has been and continues to be the basis of theoretical considerations on the editing of the multiple-manuscript text. Because of this wide use of the *Lai* as example,[3] extensive discussion is not necessary here. A brief summary of the relationships between the manuscripts, with particular emphasis on *E*, base of the present edition, should suffice.

From Bédier to the present there has been no dispute as to the principal groupings as determined by common variants: *A* and *B* form a pair, as do *C* and *G*, which are both heavily Picard and set apart from all the others in that respect, while *ABCG* in turn probably form a group to be contrasted with *DEF*. There is divergence of opinion on the status of this latter group; that is, on the relationships of *D, E,* and *F* to each other. Bédier[4] links *DF* together, with *E* by itself, while Dees[5] sees *DE* as a subgroup and *F*, the most flawed of the versions, apart. Galloway, using a computer to aid her analysis, arrives at the result that *AB* as a group is most closely linked to *E*, which she sees as standing alone.[6]

Of special importance is the fact that *E*, in almost every analysis, stands by itself. It has the fewest missing lines (only two: 674, 812) and, although its readings diverge rather often from the other six manuscripts as a group, these divergent readings are as graceful or even better than those of the other versions. Bédier[7] says of *E*: "C'est un texte d'une très belle tenue, irréprochable notamment aux 127 lieux où sa leçon lui est particulière." It is this manuscript that he uses as illustration in his 1928 monograph on the calculation of variants and establishment of filiations. In addition, he suggests that Jean Renart himself may have edited and reworked his own poem in this version,[8] a suggestion which has been received with some reservations[9] since there is no external evidence to suggest that Jean Renart, or any other author of the period, reworked his own poems in a second version known to us today. It is interesting to note, however, several lines (see notes to 194, 429-439, 815) where the reading differs from all the others and yet remains very strongly in the style of the rest of the poem.

Ms. *E* (B.N. *nouv. acq. fr.* 1104) consists of 92 velum folios, 290 x 200 mm, with an ancient wood binding covered in hide. Folios 1-79 contain a collection of *lais*, entitled on the top of f. 1r "les lays de Bretagne, cist est de Guimar" followed by a drawing, covering part of the left-hand column,[10] of a minstrel standing before a group of seated noblemen, playing a viol. On f. 79, at the end of the last *lai* is written: "Explicit les lays de Bretagne." The collection includes the *lais* of *Lanval, Desiré, Tyolet, Yonec, Guingamor, Espine, Espervier, Chievre-fueil, Doon, Dous Amanz, Bisclavret, Milun, Fraisne, Lecheor, Equitan, Tydorel, Cort Mantel, Ombre, Conseil, Amours, Aristote, Graelent, Oiselet.*

All the *lais* are in the same hand in two columns per side of 40 lines each. At the beginning of each *lai* is a painted and illuminated initial with the title of that *lai* in red. For the *Ombre* the initial *N* of *Ne* (line 1) is 6 lines high. The folios are numbered in pencil in a modern hand. Folios 80-89 are smaller in size, and in prose, 80-83, 86-89 without columns, a Latin fragment of a commentary on Job, and 84-85 in Old French in two columns, a fragment from the middle of the *Regime du corps* of Aldebrandin of Sienna. F. 90-92 are blank.[11]

*Previous Editions*

The *Lai de l'ombre* has been edited and published several times, the first of which was in 1836:

Francisque Michel, *Lais inédits des XII$^e$ et XIII$^e$ siècles,* Paris, 1836, pp. 41-81. The version is that of *A*, followed in the Appendix (pp. 125-128) by variants of *B*.

Achille Jubinal, *Lettres à M. le comte de Salvandy sur quelques-uns des manuscrits de la Bibliothèque de la Haye,* Paris 1846, pp. 154-176, where *F* is reproduced.

Joseph Bédier, *Le Lai de l'ombre* (in the *Index lectionum quae in Universitate Friburgensi per menses aestivos anni MDCCCXC habebuntur*), Fribourg-en-Suisse, 1890. The text is based on *A*, with variants from the other manuscripts except for *G*, discovered shortly afterward.

Joseph Bédier, *Le Lai de l'ombre par Jean Renart*, SATF,

Paris 1913; based again on *A* with variants from all the other manuscripts.

Joseph Bédier, *La Tradition manuscrite du Lai de l'ombre*, Paris 1929, with *E* reproduced as an appendix to the theoretical monograph, corrected 45 times, but without variants.

John Orr, *Le Lai de l'ombre*, Edinburgh 1948. The version is that of *E* with principal variants of the six other manuscripts and, as an appendix, corrections of Bédier 1913.

B. J. Levy et al., *Le Lay de l'ombre*, Hull 1977, *E* with significant variants from *A*.

Félix Lecoy, *Le Lai de l'ombre*, CFMA, Paris 1979, based on *A* with selected variants from the other manuscripts.

A new edition of the *Lai* can, however, be justified. Three of the four versions published since 1913, that is, those of Bédier 1929, Orr, and Levy, are complete for neither variants nor notes. Bédier published this first version of *E* simply as an illustration of methodology in editing Old French, without notes or variants except for some emendations where the base manuscript was manifestly incorrect. Orr and Levy both indicated that their respective editions were meant solely for university classrooms. Lecoy's edition, while more complete, is based on *A*. No fully critical edition of the poem based on *E* has been done to date, and with that in mind I have undertaken this work, for which, it goes almost without saying, I am grateful for the help and inspiration afforded me by all previous editors.

# The Story

As will be discussed below, the *Lai de l'ombre* is essentially a lovers' dialogue. It can be divided into two parts, joined by some lines of transition and preceded by a general introduction to the *Lai* and a longer introduction to the first dialogue:

## *Introduction 1-52*

Jean Renart wants to spend his time telling a pretty story, despite the unfavorable reactions of *vilains*, lowly-born people who lack in courtesy. He wants to demonstrate that happiness is more important than noble birth or wealth. The *Lai* (entitled by Jean Renart *Le Lay de l'Ombre*, the "Lai of the Shadow/Reflection") is dedicated to the Electus.

## *First Dialogue 53-585*

### *Introduction 53-310*

There was a knight, it seems without a name, who had all the fine qualities of any young gallant: he was generous, friendly, good at jousting and devoted to that sport, handsome and well-dressed. But women loved him without awakening any response in him until one day when he falls in love with a lady he had only glimpsed from afar. After reflecting on love and courtship, he decides to go present his service and love to her. He sets out with some companions, to whom he gives no explanation of the reason for the journey, and when they are near the castle of his beloved, he manipulates the conversation until his companions insist that they must pause there to pay their respects to the lady. She, who is as well endowed with all courtly perfections as the knight, has, in fact, heard of his fine reputation and gladly welcomes him.

## The Dialogue 311-585

The knight does not hesitate. As soon as his companions are seated and have begun to chat with her ladies-in-waiting, he declares his love and his great desire to serve the lady (also nameless) in order to merit her love. At first she scarcely believes that he is serious, and then she begins to regret that she had received him so courteously. She has a fine husband, she tells him, and does not want to grant her love to anyone else. Although she refuses to accept any love token from the knight, she is so moved by his ardent words that she falls into a thoughtful trance. The young man takes advantage of her inattention to slip a ring onto her finger without her being aware of it. He then breaks into her trance to say farewell, with the result that she does not notice the ring, since she is so surprised at his brusque and unexpected departure.

## Transition 586-705

As soon as the knight leaves,the lady finally does notice the ring and, both outraged and impressed by his daring, she sends one of her servants after him. The knight, not at all astonished at being overtaken by a messenger, returns willingly to the castle. In the interval she has decided to speak with him in the castle yard, at the side of a well, for, in that way, she says to herself, if he will not take back the ring, she can throw it down into the well.

## Second Dialogue 706-952

The knight is sure that the lady is now ready to accept his ring and his love, but she plans to return one and refuse the other. She does not want to expose her reputation to any risk of scandal, as she would certainly do if she accepted a lover other than her husband. She acknowledges the sincerity of his love by begging him, for the sake of that very love, to take back the ring. He finally has to recognize that he cannot refuse her demand. He states as a condition to his taking back the ring that he be free to give it to the creature he loves best after her. Curious to know who that creature is, she gives back the ring and he, after remarking that it is not hurt for having been on her finger, throws it into the well to the reflection of the lady, best beloved after her. The lady, touched by this clever action, yields her love at once. The poet leaves them there, at the side of the well, exchanging kisses and vows of love.

### Conclusion 953-962

In the last ten lines Jean Renart names himself and announces his intention of turning his thought elsewhere.

# Literary Considerations

*The Poem: Genre and Style*

Jean Renart himself twice indicated the title of his poem, the *Lai de l'ombre*, both times at the rhyme (52, 961). This is not to suggest, however, that in doing so he made precise the genre of his work, since the term *lai* does not have a fixed designation in the Middle Ages. It was, rather, not clearly distinguished from the genres of *fabliau* and *dit*.[12] At the beginning, the *lai* was a musical form of Celtic origin, but it is generally believed that the Breton or French *jongleurs* recited their tale in French before playing the music. The designation *lai* was eventually transferred to the tale itself. It is not even known if the qualifier *breton* refers to Brittany (whence bilingual *jongleurs* who sang the first *lais* for a French or Provençal audience, explaining the content in the Romance vernacular before singing), to Great Britain, or to Wales.[13]

The French poetic *lais*, which are best-known today, are those of Marie de France, dated between 1160 and 1170. It was she who determined the form for her era: brief tales in octosyllabic couplets whose subject, for Marie, is always love, either courtly or not.[14] They were composed, by contrast to their Celtic predecessors, not to be sung, but to be read or recited. They all had a prologue, a central narrated action and a conclusion, with dialogue rarely appearing except at the most important moments of the poem.[15]

With Jean Renart the *lai* can still be defined as a relatively brief narrative poem (there are only 962 lines as compared to thousands in his romances) in octosyllabic couplets. Unlike Marie de France, however, he uses dialogue as the major mode, rather than narrative or monologue. The plot is still a love story here, although, unlike those of Marie or twelfth-century writers of romances, it is very much of our world rather than fantasy, and treats love and courtship in a different, somewhat more cynical way.

This, indeed, is one of the most interesting aspects of this *lai*, described by Bédier[16] as an "historiette tendre et spirituelle, et plus spirituelle que tendre," as well as by A. Mary[17] as "plus galant qu'amoureux." What is the place of love, and of courtesy, in this poem? Bédier always viewed it as an *exemplum*, a work belonging to the didactic tradition, an interpretation accepted by G. Paris and, much later, by Simonelli.[18] What is to be taught in the *Lai* as *exemplum* is a way of winning the love of a lady. Lejeune, on the other hand, sees no teaching, but a simple tale, enriched by particularly keen observation of real life.[19] Lejeune is right, I believe, that Jean Renart was not attempting to teach, any more than Andreas Capellanus, whose *De Amore*, to which the *Lai* as *exemplum* has been compared,[20] has as its real goal that of entertaining, even through satire, the courts of the time, although it is presented as a didactic instrument.

Love, and sometimes courtly love, still plays the central role in the poem. The plot, after all, revolves around the love of a knight for a lady. The courtly tradition is respected to the extent that the knight falls in love with her from a distance; it is, in that sense, a true *amor de loin* as it had been sung first by the troubadours. He decides to visit her, and tries to win her through a love-speech, still according to convention.

But here, with his use of the ring, Jean Renart parts company with his predecessors and contemporaries. A love-pledge does indeed belong in the tradition, but not one firmly refused and then stealthily bestowed against the wishes of the recipient. Courtly love is always rational and includes, as a fundamental aspect, a great consideration for the beloved and adored lady; but here the knight refuses to respect either the reasons or the expressed feelings of the lady. There is no doubt, furthermore, that she means her refusal of his love and of the ring as a pledge; she is not being coy, but honest, in a courteous way, with her suitor.

Thanks to his trickery with the ring, the knight has made for himself the opportunity to continue his love-speech, refuted in turn by the lady until she wins: the knight can no longer insist, with any degree of consideration for her, that she keep the pledge. The amorous convention of speeches and debate has failed and the knight, if he wishes to be victorious, must find another method, not that of the courtly tradition, to become her lover.

And the cleverness of the young man here appears in its fullest strength. A gesture resolves the situation, a wordless communication which is seen to be more expedient in its total lack of worldly logic (to throw an object of some material value into a well and to refer to a shadow as a beloved creature) than a whole persuasive speech.

Jean Renart emphasizes this gesture in his title and, by this very choice of title, emphasizes his distance from courtly tradition.[21] It is not for the ring, conventional courtly pledge, that he names his *Lai*, but for the shadow, reflection of the lady, through which the knight can win her love.[22] It is tempting to see a parody of the courtly tradition here, through the failure of ordinary methods of winning a lady; but Jean Renart has also written a charming tale, indeed a love story, with a clever rather than a tender solution.

In addition to being clever, a trait which also shows itself early in the *Lai* when he maneuvers his companions into insisting that he visit the lady, and thus keeps his own strong desire to see her a secret, our hero has many other fine qualities. He is generous, modest and well-spoken, a good companion and a very skillful fighter. He knows all the games, and is as brave as he is handsome, in short a model young man. Of equal perfection is his lady, for she is beautiful, of course, and noble in character. Neither of them is named, a fact that has added support to the view of the poem as an *exemplum*, but can also be seen as a way of putting some distance between the characters and the reader. Their names are of no importance;[23] what they say and do is, almost as if we are hearing them clearly and seeing them in sharp silhouette behind an opaque curtain or screen.

*The Author and his Style*

Who is Jean Renart who signed the *Lai*? We know of his existence solely through his writing which, however, reveals little of his origins and his life. Of the three works attributed certainly to him, only the *Lai* bears his name (953). That he wrote the *Roman de l'Escoufle* and the *Roman de la Rose ou de Guillaume de Dole* was first suggested by P. Meyer in the preface to his edition of the *Escoufle* in 1894, where he also mentioned the *Guillaume de Dole* which had appeared, also for the first time, the year before.[24] Soon afterwards A. Mussafia published two studies, each one on one of these works, where he made many detailed lexical, metrical and syntactic comparisons between these two poems and the *Lai*,[25] comparisons reconsidered and confirmed in the years that followed.[26]

In 1913, as has already been noted, Bédier published his second version of the *Lai*, repeating in the preface several of Mussafia's arguments.[27] He added the solution to two anagrams which he had perceived, one at the end of each romance, each containing the name *Renart*.[28] Whether or not the existence of these puzzles and of their solution is accepted as binding proof of authorship, there is general agreement today that Jean Renart wrote at least these three works.[29]

The *Escoufle* (9058-9071) is dedicated to the Count of Hainaut, without any indication of which person bearing that title Jean Renart had in mind. The other long romance, *Guillaume de Dole* (1-15), contains a dedication to Milon de Nanteuil, bishop of Beauvais from 1222-1234. The *Lai*, although it too has a dedication (39-41), does not furnish the name of the person to whom the poem is dedicated, but designates him simply as *l'Eslit*, the Electus, an ecclesiastical title indicating someone already named bishop, but whose accession to the see has not yet been consecrated. It is tempting to identify this *Eslit* with the same Miles de Nanteuil, elected bishop in 1217 and consecrated in 1222, but it has been noted that this hypothesis, like the several specifying exactly to which Count of Hainaut the *Escoufle* was dedicated, cannot be verified.[30] There are, however, two references (242-243, 250-251) in the *Lai* to the imprisonment of Christians in Egypt, references which have been understood as a recognition of the experiences of this Miles, who had been a prisoner in Cairo during the Fifth Crusade, 1219-1220.[31]

If this reasoning is thought acceptable (always with the knowledge that absolute verification is impossible), then the date of the *Lai* can be fixed rather precisely between 1217 and 1222, the years during which Miles de Nanteuil was designated Electus of Beauvais. It is even possible to limit the dates further because of the rather indefinite reference to a Turkish captivity (243) which, if it does apply to the imprisonment of Miles, pushes the date of the poem up to 1220, after his release. Lejeune favored this hypothesis and added to it by suggesting that Jean Renart himself was in the entourage of Miles and therefore shared his journey and year in prison.[32]

Such a hypothesis, like that of the very identity of the *Eslit*, is, of course, impossible to verify satisfactorily. There is no other proof in the *Lai*, or in either of the other poems, that Jean Renart was acquainted with the Holy Lands in any way but by hearsay, and his reference at 234 to being captured by the Turks and taken to Cairo is commonplace. Lejeune, in fact, has since made a detailed argument[33] for a totally different assignment of identity to the *Eslit*. Again, it has its convincing points, but, again, it cannot be proven. As Lecoy has said in response,[34] either thirteenth-century bishop is possible, and so can be a third *Eslit* as soon as someone thinks of him!

One cannot be more precise, therefore, than the first two decades of the thirteenth century as a date for the *Lai*. It is not the place here to engage in discussion about the precise dates of the longer works, but they can both be placed in relation to the *Lai*. There is a reference, which seems deliberate, to part of the plot of the *Escoufle* in the prologue of the *Lai* (21-24), and, in the *Guillaume de Dole* (657-676), a reference to the story told in the *Lai*. The poem seems therefore to have been composed after the *Escoufle* and before the *Guillaume de Dole*.

What other information we have about Jean Renart comes from the poems. His geographic descriptions of northern France, both eastern and western, are quite exact, leading to the conclusion that he had traveled extensively or lived in that area.[35] His literary knowledge seems wide, as shown by allusions in the two longer poems to such diverse works as the *Chanson de Roland*, the *Roman de Troie*, the *Roman d'Alexandre*, the Grail legend and *Aucassin et Nicolette*. His favored comparison in all his work is between his hero and Tristan, a trait which has led Sweetser[36] to suggest that the *Escoufle* is an anti- or even a super-*Tristan*. In the *Lai*, short as it is, there are three references to that legend.

Notably lacking in any of Jean Renart's work are many references to the Arthurian tradition, the Round Table, and the works of Chrétien de Troyes. In the *Lai* there is one mention of Gawain, as the son of Lot (60-61), and none of any other knight. In addition, few of Chrétien's stylistic techniques, imitated widely elsewhere, appear here. Like the earlier poet, Jean Renart uses the interior monologue quite extensively; but other traits, especially the atmosphere of an Otherworld and the fantastic, are missing. Instead, there is what is usually referred to as this poet's realism,[37] his careful description of geography (for example, 54-57), costume (276-283), daily life (298-309). L. Foulet[38] has summed up his particular charm in his description of Jean Renart as "un fin lettré, spirituel, aimable, observateur attentif et amusé des occupations et des passe-temps de la haute société de son époque; un petit air de ne pas y toucher, un regard vif et malicieux complètent cette physionomie attrayante."

Of course the *Lai de l'Ombre* does not have the sheer length necessary for detailed descriptions of palace and town life found in the other two poems. It does, however, amply illustrate its author's ability to observe people and retain a slightly detached and amused view of what they are doing. In the description of the knight's being persuaded by his companions to visit the lady, the poet comments on the *sofisme* that he uses, the pretended innocence of any purpose. Jean Renart expresses detached amusement at the knight's trick as he relates it, as if he were not the author of the whole story himself. This detachment and amusement, in fact, when added to the cleverness of the hero's rather unusual way of courting, make up much of the charm of this *historiette*.

# Language Study

*The Language of the Poet*

## I. Versification

The *Lai de l'Ombre* is composed in octosyllabic rhyming couplets. Of the 960 lines in ms E, 11 do not contain the eight syllables of the standard line and have been emended. Two lines are missing from the complete poem of 962 lines.

For the sake of his octosyllabic line, Jean Renart makes optional the elision of the /ə/ before following word beginning with vowel in several cases.[39] The conjunction *que*, for example, does not elide at 18 *que on*, while it does at 33 *Qu'il*. As a relative pronoun it remains fully realized at 294 *cil . . . que ele/Connoissoit* and 556 *ce que*. In the same way, the particles *se* (= si) is elided (101, 260) and non-elided (240); *se* (= si, et) is elided (196) and non-elided (356); *ne* is elided (118, 121), and non-elided (493, 918).

In similar fashion, the poet varies other words for the needs of the meter: one finds both *ore* (347) and *or* (245, 448), *encore* (470) and *encor* (726), *vez* (892, 901), and *veez* (227).

Of particular note is the poet's great predilection for rich rhymes, those in which at least the preceding consonant and stressed vowel rhyme. These constitute 60% of the rhymes in the poem.[40] Many of the couplets, in addition, show more than a consonant + vowel configuration for the rhyme; there are leonine rhymes (V+ C + tonic V) of the type *dangier: vengier* (153:154), *monté:bonté* (231:232), *reson:meson* (289: 290), *parlement:durement* (703:704), and rich leonine rhymes (CV + C + tonic V) of the type *membre:remembre* (23:24), *seüe:deceüe* (529:530), *lessie:plessie* (593:594). There are seven instances of equivocal rhymes where the full word rhymes with two words consisting of the same syllables: *destruire: d'estruire* (5:6), *l'aporte: la porte* (267:268), *a mi:ami* (631:632). Throughout the poem there is evidence of Jean Renart's enjoyment of language and language games to be appreciated aurally and visually. As well as puns (see notes to 45-46, 815, 962), he uses many homonymic rhymes where the same sounds, but not the exact meaning, form couplets: e.g., *garde* (verb): *garde* (noun) (29:30), *chief* ('head'):*chief* ('end') (85:86), *preuz* ('noble'):*preuz* ('profit') (839:840). In other, perhaps more interesting cases, the rhymed homonyms are not etymologically linked: e.g., *sache* (from *savoir*):*sache* (from *sachier*) (13:14, 159:160), *deus* ('two'):*deus* ('God') (91:92), *puis* ('after'):*puis* ('well') (877:878).

Altogether there are 71 of these homonymic rhymes,[41] of which almost every one is of the acceptable form where the words differ at least in meaning. In some 5 cases a word rhymes with itself in both form and meaning, but in 2 of those some difference can still be perceived: *ot* (simple verb):*ot* (auxiliary) (63:64), *autre* (reference to a person):*autre* (reference to a thing) (185:186). The very low number of such rhymes and the fact that there are no instances at all of poor rhymes or assonance (V with V only) attest to the care Jean Renart brought to his composition of poetry.

Notable too in the poet's use of the couplet is the high percentage of broken couplets, i.e., sentences or clauses which end on the first line of a rhyme. Faerber[42] places the proportion at 60%. There are also 15 enjambements, another technique for modifying this verse form while still respecting its conventions.

II. Phonology

A. Vowels

1. *e : ie*, for instance *sens : siens* 193:194, 613:614, etc.; *pieça : despeça* 21:22. This rhyme is also found before *l*, spelled *l* or vocalized to *u*, *eulz : mielz* 403:404, *euz : miez* 197:198. *ie : ue* in one instance too, *Diex : deus* 805:806, where neither the Old French spelling nor

the Latin etyma, DEUS and DOLŌREM would suggest a rhyme.

2. *ei : ai* both in the context of [λ], *merveille : travaille* 557:558, and nasal, *repreigne : praigne* 781:782.

3. *an : en*, for instance *Tristans : tens* 457:458, *rendre : reprandre* 767:768; *blanche : vanche* 281:282 is an Old French spelling rhyme of the same sort, but here the Latin etyma are distinct, i.e., *BLANKA : VINCA.

4. In one instance the Picard trait of lowering reflexes of Latin *E* occurs at the rhyme: *vermaus : miaus* 283:284 (G. §12).[43]

5. *a : au* in *dame : roiaume* 237:238. The *u* of *roiaume* may still be seen as a reflex of Latin *L* and therefore does not affect the rhyme. *a : e* too in the pair *destrece : a ce* 779:780, where Jean Renart seems to be playing games with visual as opposed to aural language.

6. *oe : ue* in *oevre : cuevre* 671:672, both reflexes of Latin *O*. *cuisse : angoisse* 773:774, where the former diphthong is also from *O*, but the latter from *U*, both in tonic position.


B.　　Consonants

1. *c : sc, ch,* and *tc* variously, as in *destrece : gentillesce* 191:192, *teche : simplece* 539:540 (G. §38), and *leece : Qu'est-ce* 587:588. The last instance is, again, Jean Renart's propensity for playing with visual rhymes and their relationship to sound.

2. The adverb *ilues : avec* 487:488, where the final *-c* of *il(l)uec* has dropped before the generalized Old French adverbial marker *-s* without disturbing the rhyme. *s* is also found in rhyme with *z, paliz : pis* 275:276, and with *t, samit : mis* 303:304. In both these instances, it is the poet's high degree of use of rich rhyme that makes the final consonant noteworthy.

3. Postconsonantal *-r* is not included in what is otherwise a rich rhyme: *conte : encontre* 305:306.

III.  Morphology

A.  Case

1. In general there are very few case "errors" in the poet's language. At 279 is found *escureus* ('squirrel skin') as the oblique singular, rhyming with the personal pronoun *eus*, oblique plural.

2. Similarly, *merciz* (871) is an oblique singular feminine form, at the rhyme with the subject singular masculine adjective *nerciz*. It can be contrasted to the more usual oblique form *la seue merci* (906).

3. Nouns deriving from the Latin neuter normally do not show an analogical -*s* in the subject singular and oblique plural. However, there are two instances at the rhyme of *mestiers* (< MINISTERIUM) in the subject singular, 202 ( : *volentiers*) and 364 ( : *mostiers*, oblique plural). On the contrary, the oblique singular *sen* 572 does not show the etymological *s* of the stem, SENSUM, in rhyme with *sien*, also oblique singular.

B.  Pronouns

1. The Picard first person singular oblique *mi* as object of a preposition is used in the rhyme: *a mi : ami* (631:632), *devant mi : a ami* (701:702); cf. also 368 (G. §65).

C.  Verb Forms

1. The imperfect third person singular *amot* ( : *mot*, subs.) 883, is the only example of this Eastern trait either at the rhyme or in the body of the poem.

2. Three verbal rhymes show forms of Picard origin: past participles with feminine agreement (G. § 8) *trecie : drecie* (299:300) and *lessie : plessie* (593:594); imperfect subjunctives (G. § 76) *represist : mespresist* (669:670).

3. There is one Picard infinitive, *seïr* (< SEDERE) 728 (G. §17).

*The Language of the Scribe*

I.    Phonology

A.    Vowels

1. The grapheme *e* is frequently substituted for *ai* (a + yod): *fere* 19, 81 as well as *faire* 17, *plet* 146, *mes* 62 and passim. The substitution extends to first person singular verb endings, *manderé* 630, *menré* 688 as well as *parlerai* 689 and *reporterai* 885. There is one instance of *j'é* 6, as opposed to numerous instances of *j'ai* 38, 153, and passim.

2. Latin /o/ is written *ue* in *trueve* (< TROPAT) 184, *dues* 806, *ilues* 487, it can also be simplified to *e : illec* 689.

3. Latin /o:/ has developed to *eu: eure 20, seul* 155, *preuz* 110, 315. There are some instances of the grapheme *o : sor* 677, *seignor* 327, but none of closure to *u*.

4. Nasal /ẽ/ and /ã/ are usually differentiated in spelling: *langue* 14, *atant* 636, *resembler* 4, *semblant* 310, 432, *tens* 122. However, /ã/ has been substituted for /ẽ/ in *sanz* 33 (< SINE) and *fame* 149 (< FEMINA). Elsewhere, where a yod has developed, e+N and a+N have merged: *vilains* 8 (< VILLANUS), *frain* 272 (< FRENUM, mod. 'frein'), *mains* 194 (< MINUS), *estraint* 179 (< STRINGIT), *praingne* 363 (< PREHENDAT).

5. The vocalization of /l/_C gives rise to a variety of diphthongs: il > eu, *ceus* 173, 366, *chevex* 687; el > iau or eau *oisiaus* 102, *chatiaus* 227, *aneaus* 658; open ol > ou, which then may simplify to *o*. The latter simplification is a Picard trait (G. §23): *fox* (= *fous*), as opposed to *vorroie* 250, *vosist* 80, 90, 101.

B.    Consonants

1. Latin /k/>/t'/>/s/ before a palatal vowel and is written *c: cerchier* 87, *cil* 94, *ce* 111. Before an /a/, /k/>/ts/: *chastel* 225, 227, 237, *chascun* 90, 238, *chainse* 314.

2. Reflexes of ITIA vary in spelling: *hautesce* 41,

*gentilesce* 210, *servise* 118, *gentillise* 412, *gentillece* 362, 498.

3. Epenthesis is sporadic in this text, and there are more instances of forms without epenthetic consonants than with: *venroit* 242, 905, *avenroit* 807, *venront* 959 as opposed to *covendra* 951; *vorroie* 250; but *chambre* 309.

4. *s* and *z* in final position are usually differentiated; *z* < *t* or *st* + *s: doz* 79 (< DULCIS), *deduiz* 102, *tonduz* 125 (< TONDUTUS).

II.  Morphology

A.  Markers

1. There are very few errors in case marking in the entire text: *cil*, usually oblique singular, is used in two instances (540, 917) for the subject singular, usually *cis*.

2. The Picard possessive marker *vo* is found in this text, 522, 319, 577, 579, 873, as opposed to the standard *vostre* 380, 400, 524, 732, etc. (G. §65).

B.  Pronouns

1. There are two instances of Picard feminine direct object pronoun *le*, 547, 558. See also my note to lines 146-149.

C.  Verbs

1. The imperfect endings of the singular and the third person plural are the Francien forms in *-oi-*. There are no instances of the *-eve* type in this text.

2. Endings in *-iez* can be either mono- or dissyllabic in this text according to the needs of the meter. This is a standard trait of Old French; see Nyrop, *Grammaire historique de la langue française*, vol. 2, Section 1615.

3. There is one instance of the Picard future, first person plural in *-omes: feromes* 261 (G. §78).

4. Also present in one instance is the Picard present

subjunctive *messiece* 697 (G. §80).

## Place and Date of Composition

To synthesize the materials outlined above, much of the scribe's language, as well as that of the poet, show a French like that of Francien; that is, a standard literary dialect. There is nothing in the language of either the poet or the scribe (and they are very similar) to contradict the date given by other, internal, indications; everything points to the first quarter of the thirteenth century and, more particularly, 1220-1221.[44] All editors of this century have used the same reasoning in concluding that 1220 was the approximate date.

Bédier, in 1890 and 1913,[45] discussed the geographic origins of Jean Renart. As was stated above, both he and the scribe of ms. E use a fairly standard Ile-de-France dialect, though with various North-eastern traits, notably those of Picardy. None of these traits, however, are ones that do not appear on occasion in other dialects. As Foulet points out, apropos of the personal pronouns *mi, ti*,[46] "Les oeuvres des auteurs picards ont popularisé le pronom *mi*, même dans des régions de dialecte différent: on le trouve parfois à la rime dans des textes qui emploient normalement la forme *moi*." There are not enough instances of Picard traits to argue for that region as origin for either Jean Renart or the scribe. The geographic references here are sparse, but are all Eastern, and those in his other works indicate a knowledge of that area too. I would conclude, tentatively, that Jean Renart was familiar with that part of France, but his language does not indicate that he necessarily came from there or lived there for long periods of time.

## Editorial Procedures

The first goal of an edition of a medieval text is to make that text as accessible as possible to the modern audience. That much is agreed upon by all editors. Under debate, however, is the method of approaching the text: does one conflate the various manuscript readings or use what has been called the 'best manuscript' approach?[47] Comparison and conflation may lead to something closer to the author's original version, but run the risk of creating an unsatisfactory patchwork. The use of one manuscript as base, on the other hand, will more easily avoid an inauthentic result, but may obscure insights on the text which can be gained from wider use of several versions. Given the greater dangers I believe are involved in a composite text, and also because of the occasional intrinsic interest in an individual manuscript of a work with multiple versions, I have chosen to use the 'best manuscript' approach and follow ms. *E* whenever possible.

Emendations of ms. *E* have been made in 39 cases, based on omissions, obvious real errors, and judgments on clarity. The changes in the base rely on the readings of the variant manuscripts, and especially of the group *ABCG*, with *AB* particularly consulted where there is divergence within the group. Where the choice of emendation (or the reason to emend at all) is not immediately obvious, it has been discussed in the notes.

All standard abbreviations have been expanded without comment, and the octosyllabic line has been used as a norm for emendation. Morphological anomalies in the text have been changed for the needs of meter or rhyme, but not otherwise, so that, for example, of two instances of the form *ere*, third person singular imperfect of *estre* (53, 882), only one has been emended.[48]

## Notes

[1] J. Bédier, ed., *Le Lai de l'ombre, Index lectionum quae in Universitate Friburgensi per menses aestivos anni MDCCCXC habebuntur.* (Fribourg-en-Suisse, 1890), 13.

[2] Ms *G* was unknown at the time of Bédier's 1890 edition, and discovered shortly afterwards.

[3] J. Bédier, "La tradition manuscrite du *Lai de l'ombre*," *Romania*, 54 (1928), 161-196, 321-356 (rpr. Paris: Champion, 1970); all references are to the reprinted monograph. An earlier version of the same study appears in Bédier's Introduction to *Le Lai de l'ombre par Jean Renart* (Paris: SATF, 1913), xxiii-xlv. For more recent considerations of the question, see F. Whitehead and C. E. Pickford, "The Introduction to the *Lai de l'ombre*: sixty years later," *Romania*, 94 (1973), 145-156; rpt. in *Medieval Manuscripts and Textual Criticism*, ed. Christopher Kleinhenz (Chapel Hill: North Carolina Studies in the Romance Languages and Literatures, 1976), pp. 103-116; A. Dees, "Considerations théoriques sur la tradition manuscrite du *Lai de l'ombre*," *Neophilologus*, 60 (1976), 481-504; L. Foulet and M. Speer, *Editing Old French Texts*, (Lawrence, Kansas: University of Kansas Press, 1979), 18-22, 33-35; P. Galloway, "Manuscript Filiation and Cluster Analysis: the Lai de l'ombre Case," in *Pratique des Ordinateurs dans la Critique des Textes* (Paris: CNRS, 1979), 87-96.

[4] Bédier, "La tradition manuscrite," 6.

[5] Dees, "Considerations," 500-503.

[6] Galloway, "Ms. Filiation," 15-17.

[7] Bédier, "La tradition manuscrite," 66.

[8] Ibid., 67, 99.

[9] E. Walberg, "Prinzipien und Methoden für die Herausgabe alter Texte nach verschiedenen Handschriften," *ZRP*, 51 (1931), 679; F. Lecoy, ed., *Jean Renart, Le Lai de l'ombre*, CFMA, 104 (Paris: Champion, 1979), viii-ix, note 1.

[10] Folios 56 and 57 follow each other in logical order, but the modern numbering has been done in reverse, so that folio number 57 precedes 56.

[11] For further details, see Richard Baum, *Recherches sur les oeuvres attribuées à Marie de France*, (Heidelberg: C. Winter, 1968), 49-50.

[12] See, however, J. Frappier, "Remarques sur la structure du lai," in *La Littérature narrative d'imagination* (Paris: Presses Universitaires de

France, 1961), 27; J.-C. Payen, Review of Limentani, *L'imagine riflessa,* *CCM*, 18 (1975), 304. Both these critics say that one should trust the designation of genre given by the author to his work.

[13] Baum, *Recherches*, 30-31.

[14] B. H. Wind, "Idéologie courtoise dans les lais de Marie de France," in *Mélanges de linguistique romane et de philologie médiévale offerts à* *M. Maurice Delbouille* (Gembloux: Duculot, 1964), 741-748.

[15] M. P. Simonelli, "I giuochi semantico-compositivi del *Lai de* *l'ombre*," *CN*, 35 (1975), 32.

[16] SATF, ii.

[17] A. Mary, *La Chambre des dames* (Paris, 1922), xvii.

[18] Bédier (1890), 8; (1913), iii; G. Paris, Review of Bédier, 1890, *Romania*, 19 (1890), 609; Simonelli, "I giuochi," 32.

[19] R. Lejeune, *L'Oeuvre de Jean Renart* (Liège: 1935), 328; see also S. Kay, "Two Readings of the 'Lai de l'ombre'," *MLR*, 75 (1980), 515.

[20] For courtly elements in the *Lai*, see B. N. Sargent, "The *Lai de* *l'ombre* and the *De Amore*," *RN*, 7 (1965), 74-75; J. Larmat, "La morale de Jean Renart dans le *Lai de l'ombre*," in *Mélanges de philologie romane* *offerts à Charles Camproux*, I (Montpellier: C.E.O., 1978), 408-409.

[21] Kay, "Two Readings," 527, emphasizes the importance of the wording of the title of the *Lai*.

[22] Not only Jean Renart, but the rubricators of the various manu-scripts used the *Lai de l'ombre* as the title, though mss *DG* show the *Lai* *de l'ombre de* (*G et*) *l'anel*; only *F* ignores the shadow by labeling the poem *Du chevalier qui donna l'anel a la dame*.

[23] Simonelli ("I giuochi," 36-38) perceives an anagram at lines 59-64 to be deciphered as *Loth son non ot*, apropos of the hero; cf. note to these lines.

[24] Jean Renart, *Le Roman de l'escoufle*, ed. H. Michelant et Paul Meyer (Paris: SATF, 1894); *Le Roman de la rose ou de Guillaume de* *Dole*, ed. G. Servois (Paris: SATF, 1893).

[25] A. Mussafia, "Zur Kritik und Interpretation romanischer Texte, zweiter Beitrag, *L'Escoufle*," in *Sitzungsberichte der Wiener Akademie der* *Wissenschaft, Phil.-Hist. Klasse*, 135 (1896); "Dritter Beitrag, *Guillaume* *de Dole*," *Ibid.*, 136 (1897).

[26] G. Charlier, " 'L'Escoufle' et 'Guillaume de Dole'," in Mélanges . . . *offerts à M. Maurice Wilmotte*, 1 (Paris : Champion, 1910), 81-98; G. Paris, "Le Cycle de la gageure," *Romania*, 32 (1903), 487-490; F. M. Warren, "The Works of Jean Renart, Poet, and their Relationship to Galeran de Bretagne," *MLN*, 23.3 (1908), 69.

[27] SATF, vii-xvii.

[28] *Ibid.*, xvii-xx.

[29] On *Galeran de Bretagne, Du Plait Renart de Dammartin contre Vairon, son roncin* and *De Renart de Piaudoue*, all of which have been attributed, although much less certainly, to Jean Renart, see J. Orr, ed., *Le Lai de l'ombre* (Edinburgh: The University Press, 1948), xv and F. Lecoy, ed., *Le Lai de l'ombre* (Paris: Champion, 1979), xi-xii, note 1. For a recent attempt at attribution, see C. Levy, "Un nouveau texte de Jean Renart?", *Romania*, 99 (1978), 405-406, apropos of the poem "Floriant et Florete."

[30] F. Koenig, rev. of *Jean Renart and his Writings* by P. Beekman and *L'oeuvre de Jean Renart* by R. Lejeune, *MP*, 33 (1936), 319.

[31] L.-A. Vigneras, "Etudes sur Jean Renart" II "Sur la date du *Lai de l'ombre*," *MP*, 30 (1933), 357-358.

[32] *L'oeuvre*, 254-256.

[33] R. Lejeune, "Le Roman de *Guillaume de Dole* et la principauté de Liège," *CCM*, 17 (1974), 16-19.

[34] F. Lecoy, ed., *Le Lai de l'ombre*, xvi.

[35] Lejeune, *CCM*, 18-19; cf. Language Study, pp. 16-20, 22-23.

[36] F. Sweetser, ed., *L'Escoufle, roman d'aventure*, Textes Littéraires Français (Genève: Droz, 1974), xxiv-xxv.

[37] For a full discussion of realism in the works of Jean Renart, cf. C. Cremonesi, *Jean Renart e il romanzo francese nel secolo xiii* (Milan: La Goliardica. Edizioni Universitarie, 1949-1950).

[38] L. Foulet, "Galeran et Jean Renart," *Romania*, 51 (1925), 87.

[39] E. Faerber, "Die Sprache der dem Jean Renart zugeschriebenen Werke," *RF*, 33 (1915), 707-715.

[40] *Ibid.*, 701.

[41] A. Limentani, tr., *Jean Renart. L'Immagine Riflessa.* (Torino: Einaudi, 1970), 12.

[42] Faerber, 700.

[43] C. Gossens, *Grammaire de l'ancien picard*, 2nd ed. (Paris: Klincksieck, 1970); an initial G and paragraph number refer to this volume throughout the language description.

[44] See pp. 11-12 of this Introduction.

[45] 1890, pp. 11-13; 1913, pp. xx-xxii.

[46] *Petite syntaxe de l'ancien français* (Paris: CFMA, 1967), 107, §150.

[47] For general discussion of the underlying philosophy of textual edition, see A. Foulet and M. B. Speer, *On Editing Old French Texts* (Lawrence, Kansas: The Regents Press of Kansas, 1979), pp. 1-39; and C. Kleinhenz, "The Nature of an Edition," in *Medieval Manuscripts and Textual Criticism*, ed. C. Kleinhenz (Chapel Hill: North Carolina Studies in Romance Languages and Literatures, 1976), pp. 273-279.

[48]Procedure is based on the rules proposed by a committee of the Société des Anciens Textes (*Romania*, 52 [1926], 244-249). In the use of the diaeresis, I have followed the example of the *Perceval Continuations* edited by Roach (Vol. I [Philadelphia: University of Pennsylvania Press, 1949], pp. xlii-xliii).

# BIBLIOGRAPHY

*Editions*

See Introduction, pp. 1-4.

*Reviews of Editions and Critical Works*

*Bédier, 1890*

Foerster, W. *Literaturblatt*, 11 (1890), 146-150.
Paris, G. *Romania*, 19 (1890), 609-615.
Suchier, *ZRP*, 14 (1890), 244-246.
Tobler, A. *Archiv*, 85 (1890), 350-358.

*Bédier, 1929*

Hoepffner, E. *Romania*, 56 (1930), 159-160.
Levy, R. "Corrections: Jehan Renart, Lai de l'ombre," *Romania*, 58 (1932), 436-441.

*Orr*

Fay, Percival B. *RPh* , 2 (1948-1949), 338-345.
Frappier, J. *RLR*, 71 (1951), 76-79.

*Limentani*

F.B., *CN*, 30 (1970), 345.
B[aldinger], K[urt], *ZRP*, 87 (1971), 652-653.
Payen, Jean-Charles, *CCM*, 18 (1975), 304-305.

*Reviews of Critical Works*

Becker, Ph.-A., "Review of Lejeune." *ZFSL*, 60 (1935), 113-125.
Koenig, V. Frederic, "Review of Beekman and Lejeune," *MP*, 33 (1936), 319-320.


*Translations*

Goodrich, Norma. *The Ways of Love: Eleven Romances from Medieval France*. Beacon Press, 1964.
Limentani, Alberto (ed.). *Jean Renart. L'immagine riflessa*. Turin: Einaudi, 1970.
Matarasso, Pauline. *Aucassin and Nicolette and Other Tales*. Harmondsworth: Penguin Books, 1971.
Terry, Patricia. *Lays of Courtly Love*. Garden City, New York: Anchor Books, 1963.


*Editorial Questions*

Bédier, J. "La Tradition manuscrite du Lai de l'ombre." *Romania*, 54 (1928), 161-196 (rpt. Paris: Champion, 1970).
Dees, A. "La Tradition manuscrite du Lai de l'ombre." *Neophilologus*, 60 (1976), 481-504.
Galloway, Patricia. "Manuscript Filiation and Cluster Analysis: the *Lai de l'ombre* Case." In *La pratique des ordinateurs dans la critique des textes*. Paris: Ed. du CNRS, 1979, pp. 87-96.
Muller, Charles. "Les Moyens statistiques et l'attribution des textes médiévaux anonymes: à propos d'une recherche sur Jean Renart." *ACILP*, 13.2. Québec: Les Presses de l'Université Laval, 1976, pp. 633-641.
Orr, John. "Textual Problems of the Lai de l'ombre." In *Studies . . . RL Graeme Ritchie*. Cambridge: Cambridge University Press, 1949, pp. 137-146.
Paris, G. "Lais inédits." *Romania*, 8 (1879), 29-72.
Walberg, E. "Prinzipien und Methoden für die Herausgabe alter Texte nach verschiedenen Handschriften." *ZRP*, 51 (1931), 665-678.
Whitehead, F. and C. E. Pickford. "The Introduction to the *Lai de l'ombre*: Sixty Years Later." *Romania*, 94 (1973), 145-156. Rpt. in *Medieval Manuscripts and Textual Criticism*. Ed. Christopher Kleinhenz.

Chapel Hill: North Carolina Studies in the Romance Languages and Literatures, 1976, pp. 103-116.

*Criticism*

Adler, Alfred. "Rapprochement et éloignement comme thèmes du *Lai de l'ombre.*" In *Etudes de philologie romane et d'histoire littéraire offertes a Jules Horrent.* Ed. J.-M. d'Heur et N. Cherubini. Liege, 1980, pp. 1-4.

Beekman, P. H. *Jean Renart and his Writings.* Paris: Droz, 1935.

Cremonesi, Carla. *Jean Renart e il romanzo francese nel secolo XIII.* Milan: La Goliardica. Edizioni Universitanie, 1949-1950.

D[uval], A[naury]. "Jehan Renax ou Renault." *HLF*, 18 (1835), 733-779.

Frappier, Jean. "Remarques sur la structure du lai. Essai de définition et de classement." In *La littérature narrative d'imagination.* Colloque de Strasbourg 23-25 avril 1959 (Bibliothèque des centres d'études supérieures spécialisées.) Paris: Presses Universitaires de France, 1961, pp. 23-39.

Kay, Sarah. "Two Readings of the 'Lai de l'ombre'." *MLR*, 75 (1980), 515-527.

Kurkiewicz, Ewa. "La conversation galante dans Le *Lai de l'ombre* de Jean Renart." *Zeszyty Naukowe Uniwersytetu im A. Mickiewicza-Filologia*, 5 (1964), 3-8.

Larmat, Jean. "La morale de Jean Renart dans le *Lai de l'ombre.*" In *Mélanges de philologie romane offerts à Charles Camproux.* t. 1. C.E.O. Montpellier, 1978, pp. 407-416.

Legge, M. Dominica. "Toothache and Courtly Love." *FS*, 4 (1950), 50-54.

Lejeune-Dehousse, Rita. *L'oeuvre de Jean Renart.* Bibliothèque de la Faculté de Philosophie et Lettres de l'Université de Liège, 61. Liège, 1935.

Lejeune, Rita. "Le *Roman de Guillaume de Dole* et la Principauté de Liège." *CCM*, 17 (1974), 1-24.

Limentani, Alberto. "Per Jean Renart: evoluzione di una lingua poetica." *ACILP*, 13.2. Québec: Presses de l'Université Laval, 1976, pp. 947-963.

Sargent, B. N. "The *Lai de l'ombre* and the *De Amore.*" *RN*, 7.1 (1965), 73-79.

Schultz-Gora. "Kritische Betrachtungen über den "Lai de l'ombre" (ed. J. Bédier)," *Archiv*, 157 (1930), 47-62; 164 (1933) 36-50; 171 (1937), 58-65.

Simonelli, Maria Picchio. "I giuochi semantico-compositivi del *Lai de l'ombre*." *Cultura Neolatina*, 35 (1975), 31-38.

Vigneras, L.-A. "Etudes sur Jean Renart, II Sur la date du *Lai de l'ombre*." *MPh*, 30 (1933), 351-359.

Vigneras, L.-A. "Monday as a Date for Medieval Tournaments, I Apropos du *Lai de l'ombre*." *MLN*, 48 (1933), 80-82.

*Language Studies*

Faerber, Ernst. "Die Sprache der dem Jean Renart zugeschriebenen Werke." *RF*, 33 (1915), 683-793.

Kaufmann, August. *Sprache und Metrik des altfranzösischen Abenteurerromans l'Escoufle*. Diss: Göttingen, 1913.

Legge, M. D. "Le doit mainuel." In *Studi in onore di A. Monteverdi*. 2 vol., 1959; I 387-391.

Löwe, L. F. H. *Die Sprache des Roman de La Rose ou de Guillaume de Dole*. Diss: Göttingen, 1903.

Stasse, M. *Jehan Renart, Le Lai de l'ombre: Concordances et index établis après l'édition de J. Orr*. Liège: ILF/UL, 1979.

# LE LAI DE L'OMBRE

## Jean Renart

54*d*    Ne me veil pas desaüser
De bien dire, ainçois veil user
Mon sens en el que estre oiseus;
Je ne veil pas resembler ceus           4
Qui sont garçon por tout destruire,
Mes, puis que j'é le sens d'estruire
Aucun bien et dit et en fet,
Vilains est qui ses gas en fet           8
Quant ma cortoisie s'aoevre
A dire aucune plesant oevre
Ou il n'a rampone ne lait.
Fox est qui por parole lait           12
Bien a dire, por qu'il le sache;
Et s'aucuns fel sa langue en sache

---

*Rejected Readings of Ms. E:*    2 d. ainz v. (-1)—5 s. oiseus p.
—14 saucuns fox sa

---

*Variants: Title—E* Ce est le lay de l'ombre, *AB* le lai (*B* Lay) de l'ombre,
*C* Du lait de l'ombre, *D* Ci comence de l'ombre de l'anel, *F* Du chevalier
qui donna l'anel a la dame, *G* Li Lais de l'ombre et de l'aniel. 1-52 *F om.*
1 *B* me v. d. (-1), *C* Je ne v.—2 *B* d. ainz v. (-1), *C* d. ainz vorrai u., *G* d.
ainz v. auser—3 *ABDG* s. a (*D* en) el qua (*G* Ken) e.—6 *ABCG* Quar p. q.
jai (*B* ja) le, *D* q. ge ai le s. descrire (+1)—7 *ABG* d. ou en, *C* b. com dist
ou on f.—8 *B* Foux e. cil q. ces g., *G* g. f. (-1)—9 *ABDG* Se ma, *C* Se ma c.
descuevre—10 *ABCDG* A (*G* Et) fere—11 *AG* il nait r., *B* il nait parole de
l., *D* il nait cointise ne l.—12 *A* por ranposne l., *D* q. sa parole—13 *B* d.
puis q., *C* a faire p.—14 *C* f. le langue, *G* sauchūns sos se l. en lache

Par derriere, tot ce li loit,
Que nient plus que je puis cest doit     16
Faire ausi lonc comme cestui,
Ne cuit je que on peüst hui
Fere un felon debonere estre.
Et miex vient de bone eure nestre     20
Qu'estre des bons; c'est dit pieça,
Par Guillaume, qui despeça
L'escolfle et art un et un membre,
Si con cis contes nos remembre,     24
Puet on prover que je di voir,
Que miex vaut a un home avoir
Eür que parenz ne amis.
Amis muert et on est tost mis     28
Hors de l'avoir qui bien nu garde,
Et qui a fol le met en garde,
Sachiez que tost le gaste et use;
Aprés sa folie s'acuse,     32
Qu'il l'a despendu sanz mesure.
Se d'ilec avant amesure
Ses sens, sa folie entrelet
Et mesaventure le let,     36

---

15 *AB* P. droiture t. ce li doit, *C* Et par derrer tolt chou quil doit, *D* li doit, *G* d. chou con li doit—16 *A* Quar n., *BG* Car n. plus con (*G* que) je, *C* Car n. plus con je puis cest droit, *D* Noient p.—17 *D* a. grant comme—18 *CG* Ne cui je q. on puist h. (-1), *D* q. len pooist h.—20 *CG* Mieus v. (-1)—21 *ABC* de bons, *D* b. ge di p.—22 *CDG* Por g.—23 *ABCG* un a un, *G* ars—24 *ABCDG* con li—25-26 *CG* inv.—25 *B* Poez savoir q., *CG* Et puet p., *D* Puet len p. et tot por v.—26 *ABCG* Et (*CG* Car) m. vient a—27 *ACG* E. que avoir (*C* cavoir -1), *B* Sens que avoir ne que a.—28 *C* et sest on t., *D* Samis m. tost a len amis, *G* et sest tantost m.—29 *C* q. nel g. (-1)—30 *AG* Ou q., *D* a foi le—31 *ABD* Mes celui qui le (*D* tot) g., *CG* Mais cil qui tout g. (*G* degaste) et tout (*G* om.) u.—32 *ABCDG* Et apres sa (*C* la) f. encuse—33 *BCDG* Qui la d.—34 *A* diluec apres samesure, *CD* se avant (*D* prant) mesure, *G* a. samesure—35 *A* Si lait la f. qua fait, *BD* Son sens sa f. (*D* f. et) son lait, *CG* Et fait sens et f. i (*G* om.) lait—36 *ABC* Et (*B* Se ) m. li l.

55*a*  Eürs le ra tost mis em pris.
    Et por ce ai cest lai empris,
    Que je voil mon sens desploier
    A bien dire et a souploier     40
    A la hautesce de l'Eslit.
    Molt par me torne a grant delit
    Quant la volenté m'est eslite
    A fere ce que me delite:     44
    D'une aventure metre en rime.
    On dit: Qui bien nage bien rime.
    Qui de haute mer vient a rive,
    Fox est se a la mer estrive;    48
    Miex l'em prisent et roi et conte.
    Or escoutez en icest conte
    Que ferai, s'aucuns ne m'encombre,
    Et dirai ci du Lay de l'Ombre.    52
    Ci dit que uns chevaliers iere
    En cele marche de l'Empiere
    De Loheraingne et d'Alemaingne.
    Je ne cuit pas c'on tex en maingne   56

---

37 *B* Sens le ra molt t., *C* Iche lavra t., *D* Si en vueil retraire beax dis, *G* Et con le—38 *ABCG* Et p. ce lai je si e., *D* P. ce lai ge ainsi e.—39 *ABCDG* s. emploier—40 *D* A beau d.—41 *C* de mon dit, *D* h. dun e., *G* h. del delit—42 *D* M. me t. (-1), *G* M. part me—43 *A* ma v. est e., *BD* Q. sa v. ma eslite, *CG* Que ma (*G* sa) v. mest (*G* est) e.—44 *ABCG* ce qui me, *D* ce qui menbelit —45 *AB* Une a. a m., *G* Une a. m.—46 *ABD* Len d. q. b. n. et (*D om.*) b. r. (*D* rive)—48 *ABCDG* Qui a (*CG* Et au) port (*C* pont) de bien dire arrive—49 *ABD* Plus len (*D* le) p.—50 *ABCD* Or orrez par tens en cest (*C* quel) c. (*A* en monte -1), *G* Or poes par tans en cest c.—51-52 *B inv.*—51 *AG* Q. dirai sanuis (*G* se anuis +1) ne, *B* Q. dirai saucuns, *CD* f. se nus ne—52 *A* En cest lai que je faz de, *B* Que jai fait de cest l., *CG* Et (*G* Que) je faich chi du, *D* En cest dit que jai fait de—53 *A* Je di q., *B* [E]z vos cuns bons c., *C* En se dist chuns c., *D* Ge vos di cuns c., *F* Je dis uns franc c., *G* Or se dist chuns c.—54 *A* Par c. m. dengleterre—55 *C* Do L. ou dalemaigne, *D* Looreigne, *F* Lohoraine—56 *ABG* p. cuns t., *C* p. que teuls i m., *D* Ne c. p. certes cuns m. (-1), *F* p. que nulz teulz m.

De Chaalons jusqu'en Perchois,
Qui eüst toutes a son chois
Bones teches comme cil ot.
De maintes resemble au fil Lot,    60
Gauvain, si comme nos dison,
Mes je n'oï onques son non,
Ne je ne sai se point en ot.
Proesce et cortoisie l'ot    64
Eslit a estre suen demainne;
De la despense qu'il demainne
S'emerveillent tuit.  Si acointe
Ne trop emparlé ne trop cointe    68
Nu trovissiez por sa proesce;
Il n'estoit pas de grant richesce,
Mes il se savoit bien avoir.
Bien sot prandre en un leu l'avoir    72
Et metre la ou point n'en ot.
Pucele ne dame n'en ot
Parler que durement [nu] prist,

---

75 d. p. (-1)

---

57 *A* parcois, *B* Des c. dusqua pertois, *CD* chaelons jusquen artois (*D* en pertois), *F* persois, *G* jusques a pierchois (+1)—58 *ABCFG* Qui (*B* Que) si ait t.—58-59 *D* Ne cuit ge pas quil en ait trois Si preu si saige si cortois Ne qui si aient a un chois Bones t.—59 *G* B. cites comme—60 *A* m. en tret au f. loth, *BC om.*, *D* Et de m. en resanblot, *F* Comparer le vueil au f., *G* De m. restraist au filot—61 *B* Monsignour g. ce dit on, *C om.*, *D* n. lison—62 *A* M. nus noi, *B* M. ains ne peu savoir s., *CG* je ne sai mie s. *C adds* Molt par estoit de grant renon, *D* ge ne soi o.—63 *C* Mais je ne s. sil non ot (-1), *D* Ne ne sai sonques p.—64 *D* Hennor et largece et sens ot, *F* Largesce et honnour et sens l., *G* c. sot—65 *A* e. sien d., *B* e. son d., *CG* e. en son d., *DF* e. siens d.—66 *CG* la pensee q.—67 *A* Sesmerveillent t., *C* Ne veries jamais aconte, *F* Sen m., *G* Ne venries vous jamais aconte—68 *G* emparlee (+1)—69 *AG* t. ne de ruistece, *C* Ne tropuissies ne de richeche, *DF* Ne (*F* Nel) trovast nus p. (*D* de) sa—70 *A* Il nert mie de, *B* Il nert p. de trop g. hautesse, *D* Il navoit mie, *F* Il niert pas de trop g.—71 *ACDF* se sot (*C* soit) molt b., *B* se set m. bel a, *G* m. biel a.—72 *C* s. metre en—73 *G* p. ne ot—74 *CDFG* Dame ne pucele nen (*C* non) ot, *F* d. ne not—75 *AB* P. qui molt ne laint et p., *C* P. durement ne lemprist

<pre>
          N'onques a nule ne s'emprist              76
55b       A certes que il n'en fust bien,
          Car il estoit sor toute rien
          Et frans et doz et debonnere.
          Qanque chascuns en vosist fere           80
          En peüst fere entor ostel,
          Mes as armes autre que tel
          Le trovast on, plus que ne di,
          Estout et ireus et hardi.                84
          Quant il avoit l'eaume en son chief,
          Bien sot un renc de chief en chief
          Cerchier por une joste fere;
           A ce ot torné son afere              88
          Li chevaliers dont je vos di,
          Qu'il vosist que chascun lundi
          Qu[e] il estoit qu'il en fust deus.
          Onques chevalier ne fist Deus            92
          Si preu d'armes comme il estoit.
          Ce n'estoit pas cil qui vestoit
          Sa robe d'esté en yver;
          Plus donnoit il et gris et ver           96
          C'uns autres de dis tanz d'avoir,
</pre>

91 Quil e. (-1)

76 *B* Onques a n. ne cen p., *CDG* Onques a, *F* a une ne—77 *ABCFG* Bien a certes quil nen, *D* c. voir quil nen—78 *F* Tant par e.—79 *D* Et preuz et —80 *CG* en voloit f., *DF* Et (*F* Que) c. pooit de lui f.—81 *B* par o., *C* En pooit f. en son o., *D* Quanque voloit, *F* Quanquil vausist e.—83 *ACG* Le trovissiez que je ne, *BF* on que je ne, *D* t. len que ge ne—84 *B* Vaillant i estoit et—85 *CG* il ot li aume, lachee, *D* Puis que il ot le e. el c., *F* le hiaume el c.—86 *D* s. el r.—88 *D* Quar en ce ot mis s.—89 *D* c. que je, *F*. Cil c. que je—90 *CFG* Il vausist q. c. (*G* vausist c. -1), *D* Si volsist q.—91 *BCG* Quil e. (-1), *A* Quil e quil en fussent d., *F* Quil ert darmes quil—92 *ABC* Nonques (*C* Conques) c. ne fu (*C* fust) teus, *G* C'onques—93 *AB* Si peniu d. quil e., *C* p. c. (-2), *F* Plus jolis d. quil, *G* c. cil e.—94 *ABFG* ce nest (*F* niert) mie c., *C* Che nert p. chieus q. ostoioit, *D* Ce niert p. celui q.—95 *ABC* a y., *C* Ses r. deste, *D* Sa robeste en (-1), *F* en liver—96 *D* P. vestoit il—97 *B* autres dis (-1)

Et tot jorz voloit il avoir
Set conpaignons ou cinc au mains,
Ne ja riens ne tenist as mains, 100
S'en le vosist, qu'en ne l'eüst.
Deduiz d'oisiaus, qu'en li leüst,
Ama, que je ne despris mie.
Il sot d'eschés et d'escremie 104
Et d'autres geus plus que Tristans;
Molt bon mai ot un bien lonc tans
Et molt se fist amer as genz.

Il ert de cors et biaux et genz 108
Et frans et legiers et isneaus,
Et si estoit plus preuz que beaus,
Et tot ce doit chevaliers estre.
Amors, qui est et dame et mestre, 112
En ce bon point li corut seure,
Que ele en velt estre au deseure,
Et si veut avoir le treü
Du grant deduit qu'il ot eü 116
55c    De mainte dame en son aage,
N'onques servise ne hommage
Ne li fist entreues qu'il li lut.

---

98 *ABD* j. veut o lui a., *CG* Tous j. vaut (*G* volt) avoec lui a., *F* Ades vault
entour lui a.—99 *CFG* ou sis au, *D* Sis c.—100 *D* r. quil t.—101 *AB* v. que on
neust, *C* v. quon neust (-1), *D* Si le v. quil ne, *F* Que nulz v. quil ne—102 *A*
o. quant lui pleust, *B* o. se il pleust, *CG* o. quant lui eust, *D* Le d. doisiaus
que lui plut, *F* o. quant li l.—103 *ABCF* ne mespris m., *D* je nel d.—104 *C* Si
sot, *D* Molt sot, *F* Et sot, *G* Si sot descus et—105 *F* tristrans—106 *CFG*
Molt ot b. m. et (*F* un) molt l., *D* M. ot b. m. un poi de t.—108 *ACG* c. et
de braz genz (*G* et b. -1), *D* Quar il estoit et, *F* Biaux fu de bras et de cors
g.—109-110 *CG inv.*—109 *CG* f. et larges et, *F* f. et courtois et loiaux—
110 *AB* Si ert encor plus, *CDFG* Et sert encor plus—111 *ABCDFG* Tout ce
doit (*D* puet) bien c.—112 *ABCFG* q. se fet d., *D* q. fait d. (-1)—113
*ABCDFG* De ceus (*D* ce) dont ele est audeseure—114 *ABCFG* En cel (*F* ce)
bon point li (*F* le) corut seure, *D* Et en ce bon point li cort seure—115 *AB*
Ele v., *CFG* Quele en v.—116 *A* quil a eu, *C* d. quele ot, *D* Dun g., *F* Des
grans deduis—117 *C* s. aige (-1)—118 *AB* Ne ainc (*B* ains) s.—119 *AB* Ne
len f., *C* f. detreues quil, *D* e. que li, *F* f. dentrues quil, *G* Ne fist dantrues

Por ce qu'il ne se reconnut                    120
N'a son homme n'a son bailleu,
Si li fist en tens et en lieu
Sentir son pooir et sa force,
C'onques Tristans, qui fu a force              124
Tonduz comme fox por Yseut,
N'ot le tierz d'ahan que il eut
De si qu'il en ot sa pais faite.
Ele li a sajete traite                         128
Parmi le cors dusqu'au panon;
La grant biauté et le doz non
D'une dame li mist el cuer.
Or li estuet a geter puer                       132
Toutes les autres por cesti.
De maintes s'en estoit parti
Son cuer, que nule n'en amoit,
Mes or set il sanz doute et voit                136
Qu'il li covient tot mestre ensemble
Por ceste servir, qui li semble
Li rubis et toutes biautez.
Li sens, la debonneretez,                        140
La grant biauté de son cler vis
Li est, ce li est bien avis,
Devant ses eulz et jor et nuit.
N'est joie qui ne li ennuit                      144

---

120 *C* ne secourut (-1), *G* ce que ne—121 *ABCDFG* A s.—122 *B* Se il f.,
*F* Li f. elle en—124 *ABDFG* Onques t. (*D* tritans, *F* tristrans)—125 *A* c.
sot p.—126 *AB* dahan con cil e., *CDG* q. cil e., *F* le quart dahan—127 *B*
De ci quil, *CG* De si (*G* Dessi) que il ot, *D* Dusqua tant quil ot, *F* Jusques
il ot sa paie f.—128 *AB* li ot s., *CG* Amours li (*G* ki) a—129 *AD* c. jusquau
p., *CG* c. dusquau (*G* dusqual) pingnon, *F* c. jusque as penons (+l)—130
*C* le grant n.—131 *C* d. qui m. en c., *D* li maint el, *G* Chune d. li m. en c.
—132 *AB* li covint a, *CDG* li covient a (*D* tot) g. (*G* jete), *F* e. il jeter—133
*CG* p. celi, *D* p. celui—134-145 *DF om.*—134 *AB* m. en avoit p.—135 *CG*
Ses cuers q.—138 *ABCG* P. celi s.—139 *G* Li rubins de t.—141 *AB* g. doucor
de, *CG* il grans douchours de—144 *ABG* Il nest j. ne, *C* Il nest riens q.

Fors que li pensers a cesti:
De tant li a bon plet basti
Amors, qui la connoissoit bien,
C'onques nule si plesant rien                    148
Qui fame fust n'avoit veüe,
Ce dist, et s'en tret sa veüe
A garant qu'il a dit verté:
"Ahi, fet il, tente averté                       152
J'ai fet de moi et tant dangier!
Or velt Dex par cesti vengier
Celes qui m'ont seules amé;
Certes mar ai desaamé,                           156
55*d*    Fet cil, qui d'amors ert seurpris.
Or m'a Amors en tel point pris,
Qu'ele veut que son pooir sache,
C'onques vilains cui barbiers sache              160
Les denz ne fu si angoisseus."
Ce pense et dit quant il est seus
Ne ja, son vuel, ne fesist el,
C'onques mes hom en si cruel                     164
Point ne fu comme Amors l'a mis.
"Las, fet il, se je sui amis,
Que sera ce, s'el n'est amie?

---

147 A quil la—151 d. verite (+1)—164 h. einsi c.

---

145 *ABC* F. seul li, *C* a celi, *G* F. li seul p.—146 *F* li ot b.—147 *ABCG* A. qui le c.—148 *AB* Nonques n., *D* Nonques ne vi si—149 *D* Com ele estoit navoit—150 *D* d. si en t.—151 *ABF* quil dist v., *CG* A tesmoig quil dist v.—152 *AB* Ha f. il t. aversite, *C* t. kierte, *DF* tant a., *G* t. jurete (*sic*)—153 *ABCDFG* Ai (*C* A) f.—154 *D* Que v. d. p. ceste v., *G* Or vient d. por c.—155 *F* qui seules mont a.—156 *AB* mar (*B* mal) ai mesaesme, *C* ai desaamee, *F* Je cuit mar ai mesaasme—157 *ABCFG* Ceus q. damors erent s., *D* Ceus q. erent damors s.—158 *ABCG* p. mis, *D* Or la a. en t. p. mis—159 *F* Que je comperrai mon outrage—160 *ABCFG* Onques v., *D* Conques c. b. arrache (-1)—163 *D* Qui ja—164 *AB* Nonques m. e. tres c., *CG* Onques m. entre si c., *D* Conques nus h., *F* Nonques m.—165 *B* Ne f. (-1), *G* a. ma m.—166 *CG* se jestoie a.—167 *AB* ce se nest mamie, *CG* Q. seroi che sel (*G* que) nert a., *D* ce se nest, *F* Q. ferai je sel

Je ne sai ne je ne voi mie                              168
Comment je puisse vivre un jor!
Deduiz d'errer ne de sejor
Ne m'i puet mon mal alaschier.
Or n'i a fors du tenir chier                            172
Ceus qui la vont ou ele maint,
Car par ce fere ont eü maint
De lor dames joie et solaz.
Car m'eüst ceste fet un laz                             176
De ses deus braz entor le col!
Tote nuit songe que l'acol
Et qu'ele m'estraint et embrace;
Li esveilliers me desembrace                            180
En ce qui plus me delitast.
Lors quier par mon lit et atast
Son biau cors qui m'art et esprent,
Mes las, qui ne trueve ne prent!                        184
C'est avenu moi et maint autre
Mainte foiz.  Or ne puet estre autre:
Aler ou envoier m'estuet
Proier, puis qu'autre estre ne puet,                    188
Qu'ele ait merci de moi enfin
Et que, por Deu, ainz que je fin,
Qu'ele ait pitié de ma destrece,
Et que, par sa grant gentillesce,                       192
Qu'ele me gart et vie et sens.

168 *ABC* Ce ne s. je (*C* sage) ne ne v., *D* Ce ne voi ge ne ne sai m., *F* s. je
ne le v., *G* Ce ne s. ce ne me v.—170 *C* et de, *F* D. darmes et de, *G om.*
171 *AB* Ne me p. mon cuer (*B* cors) solacier, *CG* Ne me p. (*G* quier) m.
cuer a., *D* ne me p., *F* m. alegier—172 *ABG* f. de t.—174 *ABF* C. por ce,
*D* Por son afaire o.—175 *ABCG* l. amor (*CG* amors) j., *DF* l. dame j.—176
*B* Cor meust, *CD* meust elle f., *F* Quor meust elle f., *G* C. meust ore f.
—177 *ABCFG* e. mon col, *D* s. dolz b., *F* s. biaux b.—178 *C* que le col
—181 *CD* ce que p.—182 *C* L. quiert p. m. l. et a taist, *F* et si tast—183 *F*
s. gent c., *G* et emprent—184 *B* l. que trueve (-l), *F* Ha l.—186 *C* f. si ne,
*D* Molt de f., *F* f. mais ne, *G* or nen p. autre estre—187-188 *B om.*—187
*F* ou enveoir mestuet—188 *C* P. quant estre autre ne, *D* P. plus quautre,
*FG* P. quant autre—189 *ABCFG* a. de moi merci e., *D* Quil est pitie de
191-192 *ABF om.*—191 *D* a. proier de—193 *G* g. moi et me sent

Il i avroit un mains des siens
S'ele soffroit que je morisse,
S'est bien droiz que de son cuer isse     196
57a   Pitiez, et douceurs de ses euz,
Si cuit bien qu'i me vauroit miez
Li alers que se g'i envoi.
On dit: N'i a tel comme soi,     200
Ne nus n'iroit si volentiers.
On dit pieça que li mestiers
Aprent l'ome et la grant sofrete;
Puis que g'i ai parole atrete,     204
Il n'i a se d'aler la non
Dire qu'ele a en sa prison
Mon cuer, [qui] de gre s'i est mis.
Ja, devant qu'il ait non amis,     208
N'en quier[t] eschaper por destrece;
Gentilesce, pitiez, largece
La devroit a ce esmovoir!"
Il s'est atornez por movoir,     212
Soi tierz de conpaingnons sans plus.
Ne sai que vos deïsse plus:

---

207 c. de (-1)

---

194 *AB* Ele i, *CG* Elle averoit trop peu de sens, *D* Ele i a. mains (-1), *F* Quele avroit bien perdu son sens—195 *AB* je perisse—196 *C* que je seuisse, *D* de mon c., *F* Bien croi que en s. c. deusse, *G* cuer seusse—197 *AB* Doucor et pitiez de, *F* P. trouver par ses douz iex—198 *AB* Mes je c. quil (*B* que) me venist m., *CG* Mes je quit quil (*G* ki) me, *D* b. quil me venrroit m., *F* Je cuit que moult mi v.—199 *B* je i e. (+1), *C* Aler q. si je i e., *D* a. ou que gi e.—200 *AB* len d., *G* On dist quil ni (+1)—201 *B* Ne nuns, *C* Ne vos —202 *ABCG* Pieca con dist q.—203 *D* Aprent home—204 *ABCDFG* gi ai (*B* je i ai +1, *C* je ai) reson a.—205 *ABCDFG* se de laler n.—208 *A* d. quele a.—209 *AB* p. tristece, *CG* Nen ert escapes p., *DF* q. departir par d.—210 *F* G. et p. et ce, *G* p. et l. (+l)—211 *ABC* Le d. (*C* deveroit +l) a ce e. (*B* amovoir), *D* d. pitie e., *F* Que je laim mi doit bien valoir, *G* Le d. a chou movoir (-l)—212 *D* Il est a., *F* Lors sest—214 *CG* v. en die p., *D* q. gen d.

Il monte et vallet jusqu'a sis;
Il chevauche liez et pensis                         216
A son pensé et a sa voie.
Ses conpaingnons oste et desvoie
De la voie et de son penser,
Qu'il ne se puissent apenser                        220
A la reson de son voiage.
Il dit qu'il chevauche a grant rage,
Celant son pensé et sa voie,
Tant qu'il vinrent a la monjoie                     224
Du chastel ou cele manoit.
Fet li sires qui les menoit:
"Veez con cis chastiaus siet bien."
Il nel disoit pas tant por rien                     228
Qu'il montast as fossez n'as murs
Con por savoir se ses eürs
L'avoit encor si haut monté
Qu'il parlassent de sa bonté,                       232
De la dame qu'il va veoir.
Font cil: "Vos devrïez avoir

---

215 *CG* Il montent v. (*G* varlet), *D* et valt j. (-l)—216 *CDF* Et c., *G* Et chevaucent lie et—217 *AB* En s. p. et en s., *CG* Celant s. p. et sa, *F* A ses amours et a sa joie—218 *F* Senvoiseure o.—219 *ABCDG* la v. de, *F* Ses compaignons de—220 *ABG* ne sen p., *F* Il ne se puent a.—221 *AB* En la, *CFG* De loccoison (*F* lachoison) de—222 *D* Or d., *F* Dient quil—223 *A* son pensser souz sa joie, *B* p. sor sa joie, *C* En s. penser et, *D* sor pensser sor sa v., *F* son penser et sa joie, *G* En son voiage et en s.—225 *D* c. menoit, *G* u ele m.—226 *AB* q. (*A* quis) i m.—227 *A* con cil c., *C* Vooies que chiex c. s. b. Et com illuecques avient bien, *D* c. la siet—228 *B* Il nest d., *C* p. chou Ne que il acontast aichou, *F* Il ne d., *G* p. bien—229 *C* As fassez nas murs qui i fust, *DF* Qui m., *G* M. na f. na m.—230 *AB* Mes p., *CG* Fors p., *D* Tant com il fait por s.—231 *AB* Lavoit (*A* Lavroit) e. si amonte, *CG* Leust e.—232 *ABDG* de la (*D* sa) biaute, *C* la b., *F* Qui par lassaut de la biaute—233 *AB* La dame q. aloit v., *D* A la—234 *ABCFG* F. il (*F* cil) v. en devez a., *D* v. en devres a.

Grant honte, car mal avez fet
Qui ançois nos avez retret                                    236
57*b*      Le chastel que la bele dame,
Dont chascuns dit bien qu'el roiaume
N'a si cortoise ne si bele.
Or tot coi! font il, que se ele                               240
Savoit con vos avez mespris,
Il vos venroit miex estre pris
As Turs et menez en Chaere."
Il dit en sozriant: "Aere!                                    244
Or seignors, or tot belement!
Menez me un [poi] mains durement,
Car je n'i ai mort deservie.
Il n'en est nus dont j'aie envie                              248
Des chastiaus, se de cestui non;
Je vorroie estre en la prison
Salehadin cinc anz ou sis
Par si que il fust miens, asis                                252
Si comme est, qu'en fusse seürs,
Et qanqu'il a dedenz les murs."

---

246 un m. (-l)

---

235 *C* h. que m., *D* h. quar mar lavez f., *F* h. en ce ramentevoir Chevalier
qui tant quide avoir Bones teches et tant bien fait Que vous avez avant
retrait—236 *D* a. vos a.—238 *CFG* d. quen un r., *D* chascune d. que r.
—240 *AB* il quar se, *C* Et sachies bien f. il se, *D* Or tost certes f., *F* Or
sachiez bien de voir se e., *G* Or tost dient il car se—241 *G* a. mis (-l)—
243 *ABF* en (*B* au, *F* a) chaaire, *C* en caullaire, *D* en chaiere, *G* en caine
(-l)—244 *AB* s. he caire, *CG* Il prist en s. adaire (*G* a dire), *D* s. arriere,
*F* Fait il en s. aaire—245 *AB* Seignor por dieu or b., *D* s. trestot b., *F* Biaux
s.—246 *D* M. moi un poi d., *G* Me menes un (+l)—247 *DF* Que ge ni—
248 *AB* Il nest citez d., *C* Il nest n. (-l), *F* Quil nen est uns d., *G* d. jai e.
—249 *AB* Ne c. se de c. (*B* destui -l), *C* De c.—250 *D* Quar fusse ge or en
—251 *C* Salhadin c. (-l), *G* S. u c. u s.—252 *B* P. ce q., *C* f. mieus a., *F*
P. couvent que f. m. icis—253 *ABCDG* e. sen f., *F* Comme il est et quanquil
y a—254 *C* Et quanques il (+l), *F* Quentres les quatre portes a

Font il: "Vos serïez trop sire."
Il n'entendent pas a son dire                                256
Le sofisme qu'il lor fesoit;
Li bons chevaliers nu disoit
Fors por oïr mon qu'il diroient.
Il lor demande s'i l'iroient                                260
Veoir. "Que feromes nos donques?
Font cil; chevaliers ne doit onques
Trespasser n'e[n] chemin n'e[n] voie
Bele dame qu'il ne la voie."                                264
Fet cil: "Je m'en tien bien a vos,
Et si le veil et lo que nos
I alons quant resons l'aporte."
Atant guenchissent vers la porte                            268
Chascuns la teste du destrier,
Criant: "As armes, chevalier!"
A tel voiage, tel tençon!
Sou frain s'en vont a esperon                               272
Tant qu'il vinrent en la ferté

---

263 ne c. ne v.

---

255 *A* F. cil, *BD* F. cil sen s., *CG* F. cil si esteries t., *F* Vous averiez font il
tort s.—256 *A* a cel d., *BCG* Il nentendoit p. a ce (*BG* cel) d., *D* Il nenten-
dirent p. a d., *F* a ce d.—257-258 *F inv.*—257 *CG* s. ki (*G* kil) l. disoit, *D*
s. qui l., *F* Pour ce s. le f.—258 *A* c. rel d., *D* c. lor d., *F* Que li b. c. disoit—
259 *ABCDG* Se p. o. non q., *F* Et pour savoir que il d.—260 *G* l. demandent
si—261 *A* q. feriemes n., *B* q. feriens n., *CF* V. et que feriens (*F* ferons)
n., *D* V. la dame de la maison Qui de beaute a tel renon Font cil que ferion
nos d., *G* V. et ke feries vous d.—262 *ABC* F. il, *D* Par dieu c., *G* F. li c.—
263 *ABF* ne c. ne v., *G* c. ne v.—264 *AB* Ou b. d. ait quil nel v.—265 *AB* F.
il, *CG* Il dist je, *D* Font c., *F* Je me t. b. fet il a—266 *ABCG* le lo et vueil
q. n. (*G* vous), *D* Et ge le, *F* Je lo donques et v.—267 *D* se r. ne laporte
(+1)—268 *CG* A. tournent devers la, *D* Adonc g., *F* A. tornerent—269 *AB*
C. le regne del d., *D* C. les testes du, *G* t. le d.—270 *CFG* as dames c., *D* C.
les dames c.—271-272 *D om.*—271 *A* A tel voiz et a t., *CG* v. t. jouvent,
*F* v. t. chancon—272 *AB* Sor f., *CG* Sour f. s. v. esperonnant, *F.* Poignant
sen—273 *ABG* v. a la, *C* T. kil iuirent (*sic*) en la frete, *D* q. sont el chastel
entre, *F* Au chastel et sont ens entre

Il ont un novel baille outré
Clos de fossez et de paliz.
Li sire avoit devant son pis                             276
57c   Torné son mantel en chantel
Et seurcot d'ermine molt bel
De soie en graine et d'escureus.
Autretel avoit chascons d'eus                            280
Et chemise ridee et blanche
Et chapel de flors et de vanche
Et esperons a or vermaus;
Je ne sai comment fussent miaus                          284
Plesanment vestu por l'esté.
Il ne sont nul leu aresté
Jusqu'au perron devant la sale;
Chascuns vallez encontre avale                           288
As estriers par fine reson.
Li seneschaus de la meson
Les vit descendre en mi la cort;
D'une loge ou il ert s'en cort                           292
Dire sa dame la novele

---

292 ou il ere sen tort

---

274 *ABC* o. le premier b., *G* Tant quil ont le premier b. (+1)—275 *F* De
fosse et, *G* C. des f. et des p.—276 *A* son vis, *B* sires a. d. s. vis (+1), *CFG* Li
s. (*C* sires +1) a. (*C* avant, *G* avoir) d. lui mis—277 *CG* Son escut tourne en
m., *F* Son mantel tourne en *G* avoir—278 *AB* s. hermine trop b., *CG* der-
mine trop b., *F* Et sot surcot fres et nouvel—279 *CG* g. bien (*G* molt)
goutex, *D* g. et chascun dels, *F* Descarlate et de vairs entiers—280-283 *AB*
*om.*—280 *CG* Et por veoir (*G* voir) savoir c., *D* Avoit bon mantel descureus,
*F* Mout vestoit tout jours volentiers—281 *CG* Chemise r. molt (*G* molt tres
+1) b., *F* Chemise deliie et—282 *D* f. inde et blanche, *F* Chapelet ot de f.
de v.—283 *CG* e. (*C* esprons -1) dores vremaus (*G* vermeus)—284 *ABD* s.
que il f., *C* s. que je fuisse m., *F* c. il fust m., *G* s. quil i f.—285 *C* por este—
286 *A* s. nuliu a., *C* s. nulli a.—287 *A* Duquau p., *C* Dusques a p. (+1), *D*
Jusquau pignon d., *F* Jusques au p. de la, *G* Dusqua p.—288 *F* Il ni a vallet
qui ne sale—289 *AB* Aus estres p., *D* As destriers p.—291 *CG* Les voit d.
ens en la—293 *ABCDFG* D. a sa (*C* la) d.

Que cil la vient veoir que ele
Connoissoit bien par oïr dire.
N'en devint pas vermeille d'ire                           296
La dame, ainz en ot grant merveille.
Desor une coute vermeille
Avoit esté tantost trecie.
Ele s'est en estant drecie,                               300
La dame de tres grant biauté.
Ses puceles li ont geté
Au col un mantel de samit,
Avec la grant biauté c'ot mis                             304
Nature en li, ci con l'en conte;
Que qu'ele volt aler encontre,
Cil se hastent tant de venir
Q'ançois qu'ele peüst issir                               308
De la chambre i sont il entré.
Au semblant que lor a mostré
Li est il bel de lor venue;
De tant pou com ele est venue                            312
Encontre eus, se font il molt lié.
Un chainse blanc et delié

---

308 p. venir—311 de sa v.

---

294 *AG* c. le v., *C* c. venoit v., *F* c. li v.—295 *G* Connut soi b.—296 *CDG*
Ne d., *F* El ne fu pas v.—297 *ABCG* Ainz li vint a molt g. m. (*G* molt m.
-l), *F* Ne ce niert mie de m.—298 *AB* Desus u.—299 *AB* A. lues droit este
(*B* estre) t., *C* A. lues este redrechie, *DF* A. errant este t., *G* A. e. lues
retrechie—300 *F* adds: Niert pas loye a la coronne Uns chapiaux de fleurs
a corone—301 *F* de moult g.—303 *ABCFG* de samis—304 *ABCFG* b. qua
mis, *D* la b. que jai dit—305 *ABCDG* li (*D* lui) en (*G* quen) son encontre,
*F* li ot sens encontre—306 *CG* Entrestant (*G* Entretant) quele aloit e.,
*D* Q. quel v. a. a lencontre—307 *A* t. del v., *D* se hasta t., *F* Se hastent cil
si du v.—308 *CG* Que a. q. puist venir—309 *AB* Fors de la c. i s., *C* c. il s.,
*DG* c. i (*G* u) s. cil e., *F* De la sale i—310 *CD* s. qui (*D* quil) l.—311 *CFG*
est (*F* fu) molt b., *D* Lor e.—312 *AB* e. ert v., *CG* t. por che que (*G* com)
e., *F* est issue—313 *B* e. sen f., *CF* e. sen (*F* en) sont il, *D* f. cil m., *G* se
fait ele m. (+l)—314 *D* c. grant et

Ot vestu la preuz, la cortoise
Qui traïnoit plus d'une toise      316
57d    Aprés li seur les jons menuz.
"Sire, bien soiez vos venuz,
Et vo compaingnon ambedui,"
Dit cele qui bon jor ait hui,      320
Qu'ele est bien digne de l'avoir.
Si compaignon li distrent voir,
Qu'el n'est pas dame a trespasser:
Sa biauté les fet trespenser      324
Touz trois, en lor saluz rendant.
Ele prent par la main, riant,
Le seignor, sel mainne seoir;
Or a auques de son voloir      328
Quant delez li se fu assis.
Si compaingnon sont bien apris:
Assis sont, ne li firent cuivre,
Sor un coffre ferré de cuivre      332
Aveques ses deus damoiseles.
Que qu'il se deduient a eles
En demandant plusors aferes,
Lor bons sires ne pensoit gueres      336

---

316 *A* t. pres dune t., *B* t. miex dune t., *C* dune cose—317 *D* A. Luis s.—
319 *C* Et vostre c. trestuit, *G* Et vostre conpaignie andui—320 *ABCDFG*
Fet c. (*C* elle)—321 *CG* Car bien est d.—322 *C* li dissent v., *D* c. redient v.,
*F* li dient, *G* si dient—323 *ACF* Que nert p., *BDG* Que nest—324 *C* b. le
f., *D* f. nes pensser—325 *ABF* l. salu r.—326 *CG* Lors les (*G* le) p. p. les m.,
*D* m. errant—327 *CG* Li sires sel (*G* sel le +l) m., *D* s. et le fait s., *F* sel mena
s.—328 *ABCD* Or ot a., *G* Or eut a.—329 *BF* d. lui se, *G* Car dales li—
330 *G* Li c.—331 *AB* ne lor f., *C* Arriere vont ne li fissent c. (+l), *F* li font
pas c., *G* ne li fisent c.—332 *A* Sus un, *C* c. sasiet de, *D* c. covert de, *F*
Lez un—333 *AB* A. deus seues d., *C* A. aus de s., *D* A. dous gentix d., *F*
sages d., *G* A. soies d. (-l)—334 *A* se delitent a, *B* Quoi que il se delitent a
(+l), *C* se delitoient a., *D* se deduisent a., *F* Con quil entendirent a., *G* En
qui se delitent a—335 *CG* Et d., *D* Entendent a plusor affaire, *F* A de-
mander p.—336 *ABCG* Li chevaliers ni p., *F* s. nentendi g.

A eus, ainz pense a son afere.
Mes la gentil, la debonnere
Li set bien rendre par parole
Reson de qanqu'il l'aparole,                                340
Qu'ele estoit molt cortoise et sage.
Cil li met adés el visage
Les eulz por mirer sa biauté;
Molt les a bien pris a verté                                344
Ses cuers, qui s'est toz en li mis,
Que de quanqu'il li o[n]t promis
Li tesmoingnent il ore bien
Qu'il ne li ont menti de rien:                              348
Molt li plet ses vis et sa chiere.
"Bele tres douce amie chiere,
Fet il, por qui force de cuer
Me fet gerpir et geter puer                                 352
De toutes [autres] mon penser,
Je vos sui venuz presenter
Qanque je ai force et pooir,
Si en puisse je joie avoir,                                 356
56*a*   Qu'il n'est rien nule que j'aim tant
Comme vos, se Dex repentant
Me let venir a sa merci;

---

346 li ot p.—353 t. m. (-2)

---

337 *C* A liaus et bee a, *D* Encois bee a (-1), *FG* a. bee a—338 *F* La jentix
dame d.—339 *AB* p. escole—340 *B* quanquil li parole, *C* de chou quil, *F*
de quanque il (+1)—341 *ABCDG* Quele ert (*G* est) m. c. et molt s., *F* Quar
elle est m.—342 *F* Il li tient a.—343 *ABCDFG* Ses (*BF* se) iex—344 *C* a
vretet, *F* Bien les a p. a grant v.—345-346 *CG inv.*—345 *ABCDFG* q. toz
est en—346 *B* Qui de, *CG* De qanque il li ot (*G* o.) p., *F* Quar de quanque
il li o.—347 *CG* Li tesmoignoit ore molt b., *F* Lors tesmongne il—348 *CG*
Que ne—349 *B* p. son v., *G* p. son bel v. et (+1)—350 *ABF* d. dame c.—
351-352 *F om.*—351 *CD* Fait cil p.—352 *D* Ma fait g.—354 *G* Je vous v. (-1)
—355 *F* Tout mon service et mon p.—356 *F* Quar se dieux me doinst j.
357 *C* n. qui jaim, *D* r. que ge a. autant, *F* Il nest nule que jaime t.—358 *DF*
Con v. se d. par (*F* vrai) r.—359 *D* l. a bone fin venir

Et por ce sui ge venuz ci         360
Que je veil que vos le sachiez
Et que gentillece et pitiez
Vos en praigne, qu'il est mestiers
Que, qui en feroit as mostiers     364
Oroison, si feroit il bien,
Por ceus qui n'entendent a rien
S'a estre non loial ami."
--"A, sire, por l'ame de mi,      368
Fet ele, qu'avez vos or dit?
Molt me merveil! Dont sifet dit!"
--"Dame, fet il, je vos di voir.
Vos toute seule avez pooir       372
Sor moi plus que dame qui vive."
La colors l'en croit et avive
De ce qu'il dit qu'il est toz sens.
Puis li a dit par molt biau sens:    376
"Certes, sire, je ne croi mie
Que si biaus hom soit sanz amie
Con vos estes; nus nu creroit.
Vostre pris en abesseroit,       380
Et si en vaurïez molt mains.
Si biaus hom de cors et de mains,

---

369 ore dit (+1)

---

360 *A* Que p., *G* Por cho s. jou v. ichi—361-364 *B om.*—362 *A* Que gentelises et p., *C* Vir se g., *D* Que g. et p. (-1), *G* Et gentilleces et p.—364 *DF* au m.—365 *C* O. li f.—366 *CG* q. ni e. r.—367 *C* Fors a e., *G* Fors e. vrai l.—368 *FG* He s.—369 *C* ore dit (+1), *D* e. por quavez ce d., *F* F. cele quavez ore d., *G* que aves v. d.—370 *ABCG* Se diex me lest veoir lundit, *D* Dame fait il se diex maist, *F* Foi que je doi saint esperit—371 *C* D. fait je v. (-1), *D* Sachiez de fi ge v., *F* fet cil je di tout v.—373 *ABCFG* que fame q.—374 *B* c. la crout et, *CDF* c. li croist et, *G* Lors li monte colors et a. (+1)—375 *C* quil ert s. (-1), *F* A cest mot quil, *G* d. que il est s.—376 *ABCG* Apres a (*CG* li) dit par m. grant s., *D* Enpres a, *F* Fet elle aprez p. m. grant s.—378 *ABCDF* si preudon s., *G* si fais h.—379 *CG* C. iestes nus ne le querroit, *F* Que v. e. n. ne querroit—381 *F* Et vous en v.—382 *ABF* de braz et

De braz et de toute autre rien,
Vos me savrïez ja molt bien     384
Par parole par mi l'ueil trere
La plume, et ce c'on ne doit fere
Fere a entendre, par verté."
Bien l'a en son venir hurté     388
Par parole et desfet son conte,
Si con cil qui m'aprist le conte
Le m'a fet por voir entendant.
Il se sueffre a mener tendant,     392
Qu'il n'estoit riens que tant amast;
S'uns autres le mesaamast,
Il s'en seüst bien revengier,
Mes il ert si en son dangier     396
*56b* Qu'il ne l'osoit de rien desdire,
Ainz li recommença a dire:
"Ha, dame, merci, por pitié!
Vostre amors m'a fet sanz faintié     400
Descovrir les max que je sent.
Molt mal s'i acorde et asent
Vostre parole a vos biax eulz,
Qui m'acueillirent orains mielz     404

---

383 *AB* De cors et, *DF* Et de b. (*F* cors) et de tote r.—385 *ACDG* p. et par lui (*C* par oeil) atrere (*CDG* traire -1), *B* p. et par la trere (-1), *F* Une plume traire par lueil—386 *ABCDG* La pene et (*CG* a) ce que ne (*C* je) vueil f., (*C* taire), *F* Et ce quidier que je mains v.—387 *ABCDG* A e. p. (*G* por) verite, *F* F. entendant p. verite—388 *F* Moult la, *G* La en (-1)—389 *F* De p. —391 *CG* Le me f.—392 *D* se suevre m., *F* Cest ce quil maine plus t.— 393 *B* Il nestoit, *C* Car il nest r. que il t. (+1), *D* Que nestoit, *G* Car il nest r. ki t.—394 *ACFG* Sune autre li (*F* le) m., *B* Sune a. le mesamast (-1)— 395 *CDG* sen (*D* se) s. molt b. vengier—396 *ABCG* il est si, *D* il est tant en— 397-398 *G inv.*—397 *ABCFG* ne lose de—398 *ABCG* Puis li r. (*G* recommenche -1), *F* Lors li ra commencie a—399 *CF* d. fait il p.—400 *C* me fait s. faintisse, *F* Fine a. me f., *G* a. me fait—401 *F* D. le mal q.—402 *CG* m. sacorde et (-1), *D* Mon mal, *F* Malement sacorde et—403 *AB* p., et voz, *C* v. dous iex, *G* v. ·ii· iex—404 *AB* macueillirent jehui miex, *F* Moult macueillirent

Au venir, et plus plesamment.
Or sachiez bien certainement
Ce fu cortoisie qu'il firent,
Car tres l'eure qu'il primes virent,            408
Ne virent nul, ce est la some,
Qui si se vousist a vostre home
Tenir, con je veil sanz faintise.
Douce dame, par gentillise,                      412
Car le vos plese a essaier:
Retenez moi a chevalier
Et, qant vos plera, a ami,
Car, ançois un an et demi,                        416
M'avrez vos fet si preu et tel
Et as armes et a l'ostel,
Et tant de bien en mon cors mis,
Que li nons c'on apele amis,                      420

Se Diex plet, ne m'iert ja veez!"
--"Le cuidier que vos i avez,
Fet ele, vos en fet grant bien.
Je n'entendoie au regart rien                     424
Se cortoisie non et sens,
Mes vos l'avez en autre sens

406 *AB* Et s., *CG* Et bien s.c.—407 *ABCG* Que courtoisie (*C* courtoisient *sic*) fu quil, *D* Que molt grant c.—408 *AB* Quar des lors que il p., *CG* Certes leure qui (*G* quil) premiers v., *D* leure que p., *F* Quar puis leure—409 *AG* Nen v., *C* Moi nen v. n. cest la, *D* Nen v. il nul cest la, *F* Que regarderent cest la—410 *DF* se tenist a—411-418 *F* The first letters of each line are missing.—411 *D* Si comme ge faz s., *F* . . . je fais et s.—412 *A* d. vo g., *B* d. na g., *D* De ce dame, *F* . . . ce dame—413 *A* a otroier, *B* c. vous p. se a otroier (+1), *F* . . . il v. p.—414 *C* Reteneme a vo c., *G* Retenes a vo c., *F* . . . moi—415 *F* . . . ant vous—416 *AB* Ainz que past un an (*B* past an -1), *CG* Et a., *F* . . . ois un—417 *CG* fait et p., *F* . . . vous—418 *C* a hostel, *F* . . . mes et—419 *ABD* Et tant avrez bien en moi m., *CG* t. ares vous en moi m., *F* Et avrez en moi tant bien m.—420 *C* Quelt nous con appiellen a. (*sic*), *F* Q. cis n.—421 *D* ne messera donez—422 *ABFG* v. en a.—423 *ABCDFG* e. apres vous f.—426 *AB* a. assens, *F* Et v.

Noté folement, si m'en poise.
Se ge ne fusse si cortoise,                                         428
Il m'en pesast ja durement;
Mes il avient assez sovent
Quant aucune dame vaillant
Fet aucun chevalier semblant                                       432
De cortoisie et d'ennor fere,
Lors cuident tot lor autre afere
Cil soupirant avoir trové.
Par vos l'ai ge bien esprouvé;                                     436

56c       Tout ainsi l'avez entendu.
Miex vos venist avoir tendu
La hors une roiz a colons,
Que, se li ans estoit si lons                                      440
Et li demis con troi entier,
Ne savrïez tant esploitier,
Por riens que vos seüssiez fere,
Que je fusse ausi debonnere                                        444
Envers vos con j'estoie orainz.
Li hom se doit bien garder ainz

427 *AB* N. comme fols si, *C* Tourne f., *G* si me p.—429 *ABD* ja molt vers vous, *CG* Il men (*G* me) peseroit ja vers vous, *F* men corcaisse ja vers vous—430 *ABCFG* Por cest (*F* ce est +1, *G* ceste +1) fole chose de nous (*G* vous), *D* Molt est fole chose de nos—431 *ABCG* Dames qui sons (*BG* sont) mal parcevanz, *D* Dame si mal aparcevanz, *F* Dames et moult mal percevans—432 *ABCG* Quant cortoisie et biaus samblanz, *DF* Quar quant amors (*F* parole) et (*F* ou) biel semblant—433 *ABCDFG* Nous (*B* Les) maine a cortoisie fere—434 *B* t. lautre a. (-1), *CG* L. i c. (*G* L. c. -1) un a., *D* Dont quident, *F* Errant c. t. lautre a.—435 *B* C soupirent *CG* C soupriant—436 *C om.*, *F* A vous—437 *AB* Ausi lavez vous e., *C* Par vous lai ge bien e., *DFG* Quainsi (*G* Ensi) lavez vous e.—438 *F* Vous avez en tel leu t.—439 *ABCG* r. aus c., *D* Ou as biches ou as c., *F* Certes si comme nous cuidons—440 *ABCDG* Quar se, *F* e. plus l.—441 *C* d. contre t. (+1), *F* d. que t.—442 *ABG* s. vous t., *C* Ne saveries t (+1), *F* Ne porriez vous e.—443 *D* De riens, *F* v. peussiez f.—444 *ABCDFG* f. si d.—445 *AB* c. je fui o., *C* c. je estoie (+1), *D* jestoie hui main, *F* Vers v. comme jestoie, *G* E. con (-1)—446 *F* On se d. moult b.

Qu'il se vant de chose qu'il n'ait."
Or ne set cil, n'en dit n'en fait,                    448
Qu'il puist fere ne devenir:
"Au mains n'en puis ge pas venir,
Dame, fet il, que j'ai esté.
Pitié et deboneretté                                   452
A il en vos, je n'en dout mie,
N'onques ne failli a amie
Nus en la fin qui bien amast;
Si me sui mis en mer sanz mast                         456
Por noier aussi con Tristans.
Comment que j'aie esté lonc tens
Sires de ma volenté fere,
A ce ai torné mon afere                                460
Que, se je n'ai merci anuit,
Ja mes ne cuit que m'i anuit
Nule, quant g'istrai de cesti.
Un tel plet m'a mes cuers basti                        464
Que en vos s'est mis sanz congié."
En faisant un petit ditié,
Fet ele, "Ainz mes tele n'oï!

---

447 *ABD* se lot de qui il le fet, *CG* Kil (*G* Qui) saiche de qui (*G* cui) il se
fet, *F* Con se vit a qui on le fet—448 *A* c. en d., *B* d. ne f., *C* s. il ne d. ne
f., *D* c. en d. ne en f., *F* Or ne voit c. en d. n., *G* set il nen—449 *G* Qui p.—
450 *AB* m. ne p. je p. faillir, *CG* m. ne doie p., *DF* nen (*F* ne) doi ge p.—
451 *C* il con jai—452 *CG* P. ne d., *F* P. ou d.—453 *AB* v. nen (*B* ne) doutez
m.—455 *B* Nuns en, *F* En la f. nulz q.—456 *CF* Je me s. m. en m. (*F* et met)
s.—457 *C* P. voir a. comme t., *F* c. tristrans, *G* P. veoir a. con t.—458 *D*
Combien que ge aie (+1)—460 *B* ce atorne m., *CG* A el ai—461 *F* Se vous
nen prent pitie a.—462 *AB* que il manuit, *C om.*, *D* Ne quit james quele
maist, *F* q. men a., *G* Ja ne c. mais que nus manuit—463 *C* q. je isterai de
(+1)—464 *C* p. mes cuers me b., *D* ma amors b., *G* plaist a m.—465 *ABCG*
Qui en, *B* v. est m., *C adds:* Dont je ai molt men cuer blechie  En faissant
un petit risset  Molt plaisant et molt netelet  Et molt avenamment li sist
Dont mes cuers molt sen esjoist, *F* Quil sest mis en vous s.—466 *AB* Un
petit en fesant ris gie, *D* p. congie, *FG* p. ris gie—467 *A* e. ainc m., *C* Certes
fait cele ains noi, *F* e. onques m. tel noy

Or puet bien demorer issi,                           468
Puis que voi que n'est pas a gas;
Encore, par saint Nicolas,
Cuidoie que vos gabissiez."
—"Certes, dame, se vos fussiez                       472
Une povre garce esgaree,
Bele douce dame anoree,
Ne m'en seüsse je entremetre."
Que qu'il puist dire ne prometre,                    476

56d    A ce ne li puet rien valoir
Qu'il en doie ja joie avoir
De li, si ne set que il face.
Li vermaus li monte en la face                       480
Et les lermes du cuer as eulz,
Si que li blans et li vermeulz
Li moille contreval le vis.
Or est il bien la dame avis                           484
Ne li fausse pas de couvent
Ses cuers, ainz set bien que sovent
L'en sovient il aillors qu'ilues.
Certes, s'ele plorast avec,                           488
La dame molt fesist grant bien;

---

468 *BCDG* d. ainsi, *F* Il p. b. remanoir ensi—469 *ABCD* q. je voi que ce est
gas (*C* est a gas +1), *F* Quant joi que cest, *G* que cho est a—470 *D* Cuidoi
ge p.—471 *CG* que me g., *D* Encor que vos v., *F* Cuidai je q.—472 *A* En
non dieu d. se f., *B* En non dieu ne se, *CG* En non dieu fait il se, *D* En non
mes se, *F* E non dieu nai se—473 *CG* Une fole g. e. (*C* esgree -1)—474 *ABF*
B. gentiz d.—475 *D* men deusse ge, *F* s. jentremetre—476 *ABCDFG* Riens
quil (*B* qui) p.—477 *ABCDG* Ne li puet a ce r., *F* Ne li puet aidier ne v.—
478 *AB* Que il puisse ja, *CG* Que ja en doie joie, *D* Que il ja joie doie a.,
*F* A enterine joie a.—479 *AB* s. quil en f., *CG* li se ne (*G* nen) s., *D* De
lui sil ne, *F* Pour ce quil ne s. quil en f.—480 *D* li cort a la, *G* v. ki m.—
483 *ABF* Len m., *CG* m. tout aval le, *D* Len cole c.—485 *F* li faille point
de—486 *F* Ains voit elle b.—487 *AB* Len semont il, *F* a. que luec—488
*ABCD* C. sor en p., *F* C. sore p., *G* C. sor emporast a. (*sic*)—489 *AB* m. li
feist bien, *CDG* m. par f. b.

Ele ne cuidast ja por rien
Qu'il deüst estre si destroiz.
"Sire, dist ele, n'est pas droiz    492
Que je aimme vos ne autre home,
Que j'ai mon seignor molt preudome,
Qui molt me sert bien et enneure."
–"Ha dame, fet il, a bone eure!    496
De ce doit il estre molt liez.
Mais [se] gentillece et pitiez
Vos prenoit de moi et franchise,
Ja nus qui d'amors chant ne lise    500
Ne vos en tenroit a pieur,
Ainz ferïez au siecle honeur,
Se vos me volïez amer;
A une voie d'outremer    504
Porrïez l'aumosne aatir."
–"Or me fetes de vos partir,
Sire, fet ele, c'est plus let!
Mes cuers ne m'i sueffre ne let    508
Acorder en nule maniere;

---

498 Et gentillece et p. (-1)

---

490 *D* Quele ne, *F* El ne c. pour nulle r.—491 *CG* Que sil (*G* si) d. iestre d.,
*F* Quil peust e.—492 *ABDF* Fet ele sire nest, *D* e. il nest—493 *ABCFG* Par
(*G* Por) dieu (*F* Certes) que jaim ne vos ne h.—494 *AB* s. et p., *CG* s. mon
p., *D* Jaime m. s. mon p.—495 *F* Qui forment me s. et, *G* Qui m. bien me
s. et—496 *D* d. se dieu me sequeure, *G* d. dist il bone e. (-1)—497 *ABDF* Par
foi (*F* Certes) ce d. il e. l., *CG* Par foi molt en doit e. l.—498-502 *F The last
letters of each line are illegible.*—498 *D* Et gentillece et p. (-1), *AB* Se
gentelises et p., *F* et p . . .—499 *B* V. prendroit de, *CG* m. enfranchir,
*F* et . . .—500 *CG* cante et list, *F* dam . . .—501 *D* t. au peor, *F* tenroit . . .
—502 *AB* A. en f., *D* A. en feroit, *F* f. au . . ., *G* A. me f.—503 *B* me volez
a. (-1), *CG* me daingnies a.—505 *ABFG* En p., *C* Lempories, *D* En porrez
(-1)—506 *D* me ferez de, *F* Vous me ferez de v.—507 *AB* e. cestroit l., *C*
e. siert molt l., *DG* f. (*G* dist) e. sert p., *F* Ce dist la dame siert p.—508
*ABCDG* ne me s., *F* mi veult ne ne

Por ce, s'est oiseuse proiere,
Si vos proi que vos en soufrez."
--"Ha, dame, fet il, mort m'avez!                      512
Gardez nu dites mes por rien,
Mes fetes cortoisie et bien:
Retenez moi par un joel,
Ou par çainture ou par anel                            516

58a     Ou vos recevez un des miens,
Et je vos creant qu'il n'iert biens
Que chevalier face por dame,
Se j'en devoie perdre l'ame,                            520
Si m'aït Dex, que je ne face.
Vo douz vis et vo clere face
Me püent de pou ostagier;
Je sui toz en vostre dangier,                           524
Qanque je ai force et pooir."
--"Sire, je ne veil pas avoir,
Fet la dame, le lox sanz preu.
Bien sai c'on vos tient a molt preu,                    528

---

513 nu fetes m.—515 Recevez m.—517 v. retenez un—521 je nen f.

---

510 *C* sest wisseuse parole et p. (+3), *D* ce est o.—511-512 *ABCG* Ha dame
fet (*CG* dist) il mort mavez Se vous de moi merci navez—511 *D* v. mens s.—
512 *D* Hai f. il m. mavriez (-1)—513 *ABCDG* G. nel d. m. (*C* pas, *G* ja)
p., *F* Pour dieu ne d.—515 *G* R. par moi un—517 *F* v. en prendez un—518
*ACG* nert (*CG* nest) riens, *B* que niert riens, *D* Quar il est courtoisie et
b.—519 *F* c. doie p.—520 *D* p. mame, *F* Faire se jen devoir lame, *G* Se ie
d.—521 *CG* Douce dame q., *D* Enz en la fin q., *F* Perdre en fin q. je ne le
f. (+1)—522 *AB* Vo vair oeil et, *CG* Vo douch oel et, *D* Vostre d. v. vos
c., *F* Vos clers v.—523 *AB* Me puet de molt poi justicer, *CG* Me porront
(*G* poroit) de (*C* par) poi justicier, *D* Ne me puet de, *F* Me poroit pour
p. estanchier—524 *AB* Je ai t. souz (*B* caus) v., *CG* Car je s. sous (*G* sor)
v., *D* Ge met t., *F* Que vous avez tout sans d.—525 *AB* Quanques je (*B*
jen) ai, *F* Q. jai et cors et avoir—526-530 *F* The first letters of each line
are illegible.—526 *BC* je nel v., *DF* ge nen v., *F* . . . ire—527 *ABD* F. ele
le l. s. le p., *CG* Dist elle le (*C* se) l. s. le p., *F* . . . lle le l.—528 *F* . . . con,
*G* t. molt a p.

Et s'est pieça chose seüe.
Bien seroie ore deceüe,
Se ge vos metoie en la voie
De m'amor et je n'i avoie                          532
Le cuer: ce seroit vilenie.
Il est une grant cortoisie
D'issir hors du blasme qui puet."
--"Dire tot el vos en estuet,                       536
Dame, fet il, por moi garir.
Se vos me lessïez morir
Sanz estre amez, ce seroit teche,
Se cil biaus vis plains de simplece               540
Estoit omecide de moi.
Il en covient prendre conroi
Prochain en aucune maniere.
Dame de biauté et maniere                          544
De toz biens, por Deu, gardez i!"
Cil biau mot plesant et poli
Le font en un pensé choïr
D'endroit ce qu'ele velt oïr                       548
Sa requeste et s'en ot pitié.
El ne le tient mie a faintié,
Les soupirs, les lermes qu'il pleure;

529 *C* choseue (-1) *F* . . . ca—530 *CG* Molt s. (*G* seroit) o., *D* Molt seraie
o., *F* . . . moult deceue—531 *A* Se or v., *B* Sor v. (-1), *D* m. a la—532 *C* je
navoie (-1)—533 *C* ce seront v.—534 *C* Il fait u.—535 *ABCFG* Dissir fors de
b.—536 *F* Ha dame tout el v. estuet—537 *D* il moi (-1), *F* Dire f.—538 *B*
l. ci m., *CG* l. or m., *D* v. mi l.—539 *CG* e. amis che sera t., *D* Por e.—540 *BG*
Se cist (*G* cis) b., *C* chius b. v. p. de simple (-1), *D* Que si b., *F* Se vos dous
v.—542 *B* c. preconroi (-1), *CG* Vous en—543 *AB* De moi en—544 *CG* b.
en m., *F* et lumiere—545 *D* d. penssez i—546 *C* b. plaisant oeil et, *F* Cil
douz m., *G* C. bel oel p.—547 *CG* Me f. en un (*G* en vo) p., *D* La f. en un
endroit c.—548 *D* De ce que ele v., *F* Endroit ce que ne v.—549 *ABCG* r.
sen ot, *F* sen a p.—550 *ABD* Quar ne (*D* nel) tient (*A* tint) a point de f.,
*CG* Car ni entent point de pitie (*G* de f.), *F* Quar ne t.—551 *CG* As s. nas l.,
*G* l. qui p.

Ainz dit que force li ceurt seure      552
D'Amors, qui tot ce li fet fere,
Ne que ja mes si debonnere
Ami n'avra, sel n'a cestui;
Mes [ce] que onques mes fors hui      556

58*b*    N'en parla li vient a merveille.
Avec ce penser le travaille
Resons, qui d'autre part l'opose
Qu'ele se gart de fere chose      560
Dont ele se repente au loing.
A celui qui ert en grant soing
Du penser ou ele ert entree
A mont bele voie mostree      564
D'une grant cortoisie fere
Amors qui en tant maint afere
A esté voiseuse et soutille.
Entrus que estoit la gentille      568
Ou grant penser ou elle estoit,
Cil tret erranment de son doit
Son anel, si l'a mis el sien.
Puis fist aprés un greignor sen,      572
Qu'i li derompi son penser,

---

556 Mes que (-1)—562 De c.

---

552 *D* Et d., *F* Lors d.—554 *CG* Et q. ja m. si (*G* li) d., *D* Ne jamais nul si—
555 *ABCG* navra se (*G* si) na—556 *B* ce quonque (-1), *C* m. ne h., *D* M. de
ce conques, *F* m. que h., *G* o. fors ke lui—557 *AB* li vint a, *C* len vint a m.
(*sic*)—558 *AB* A. cel pensse (*B* pencer), *CDG* p. se t., *F* p. la t.—559 *C* R.
que dautre, *D* Amors q.—561 *G* r. a lonc—562-565 *ABCG om.*—562 *D* De
c. q. est en—564 *F* A trop b.—565 *D* De molt g.—566 *ABCG* m. (*C* mal)
besoing, *D* qui entent m., *F* en maint tel a.—567 *AB* e. sages et, *D* e. cortoise
et—568 *ABCDG* E. quele estoit la (*C* li, *G* si) g., *F* En ce quele e.—569 *AB*
El pensser la ou, *CG* El p. de la u estoit, *F* El p. ou e. entendoit—570 *AB*
Si t., *CG* Il a trait laniel de, *F* Trait cil e.—571 *ABDF* S. (*F* Un) a. se li mist
el s., *CG* Eranment si la m. (*G* li mist) el—572 *ABCG* De ce fist il un (*CG*
que) molt grant s. (*CG* bien), *D* Apres a fait ausi grant s., *F* Si fist a.—573
*ABCG* Si ert (*G* est) sousprise del p., *F* Quil li rompi lues s.

Que ainz ne li lut apenser
De l'anel qu'ele avoit el doit.
A ce qu'ele ne s'en gardoit,        576
"Dame, fet il, a vo congié!
Sachiez que mon pooir et gié
Est toz en vo commandement."
Cil se part de li erranment,        580
Et si conpaingnon ambedui;
Nus ne set la reson, fors lui,
Por qoi il s'en depart issis.
Il fu soupiranz et pensis,        584
Venuz est au cheval, si monte.
Fet cele a qui le plus en monte
De lui remetre en sa leece:
"Iroit s'en il a certes? Qu'est ce?        588
Ce ne fist onques chevaliers!
Je cuidasse c'uns anz entiers
Li fust assez mains lonc d'un jor,
Por qu'il fust o moi a sejor,        592
Et il m'a ja si tost lessie.
Ahi! S'or m'i fusse plessie
Vers lui de parole ou de fet!

---

574 *A* Q. ainc ne, *B* Quains ne (-1), *CG* Onques ne, *D* Conques ne, *F* Quil ne li leust a.—575 *AB* quele ot en son d., *G* a. en d.—576 *ABD* quele mains se (*D* sen) g., *C* Que quelle mains si se g., *F* Et quant elle mains sen, *G* Et quele mains se regardoit—577 *CG* D. dist il, *F* Si dist cil or men irai gie—578 *D* m. penser et, *F* Ma douce dame a vo congie—579 *F* Et t.—580 *ABF* Il se, *CG* Lors se, *D* Si sen p.—581 *F* Ains ni fist plus darrestoison, *G* c. avuec lui—582 *ABCDG* s. lachoison f., *B* Nuus ne, *F* Nulz fors lui ne set lachoison —583 *ABCG* p. quil (*C* quoi) sen (*CG* en) est ainsi partis, *D* il se d. ainsis, *F* sen aloit ensi—584 *ABCDFG* Il est s.—585 *ABCF* V. a son c., *G* e. a son c. (+1)—586 *A* Et c., *B* A c., *CG* Dist c. (*G* ele) a cui p. en amonte—587 *F* De lui remetre (-4)—588 *B* c. quesce, *CG* Ira sen il (*G* il sent) a c. quesse, *F* I. sent il a c. quesce—590 *CFG* Je cuidoie cuns (*C* cis) a.—591 *AB* m. cors dun—592 *ABF* Mes quil f. o (*F* lez) m., *C* Puis quil—594 *AB* A. se mi, *C* A. se me f., *F* sor me f., *G* A. se je f. baissie—595 *D* Envers lui en dit ne en f., *F* l. en p. ou en f.

58c

Por les faus semblanz qu'il m'a fet          596
Doit on mes tot le mont mescroire.
Qui por plorer le vosist croire
Et por fere ses faus soupirs,
Si me consaut li Sains Espirs,          600
Ja por ce n'i perdist il rien.
Nus ne guilast ore si bien
Ne si bel, ce est or du mains."
Atant envoie vers ses mains          604
Un regart, si choisi l'anel;
Toz li sans dusqu'au doit manel
De son pié li esvanoï.
N'onques mes si ne s'esbahi          608
Ne n'ot de rien si grant merveille.
La face qu'ele avoit vermeille
L'en devint trestote enpalie:
"Qu'est ce? fet ele, Dex aïe!          612
Je voi ci l'anel qui fu siens.
De tant sui je bien en mon sens
Que je vi orains en son doit

---

597 m. meins croire (*sic*)—606 d. manmel

---

596 *B* Par l., *D* f. soupirs quil a f., *G* kil a f.—597 *ABD* Doit len m., *CG* On doit m.—598 *F* Certes qui or le—599 *ABCG* Ne p. f. s. (*CG* les) f., *F* Pour plourer ne faire s.—600 *AB* c. sainz esperis, *CD* s. espris—601 *ABCG* Por ice ni (*C* ne) p., *F* Por ce ne p. il ja r.—602 *B* Nuns ne, *C* N. nen gilla o., *D* Onques nul jor nen fu si, *G* Ne nen g.—603 *ABCFG* b. cest ore du, *D* b. com e.—605 *ABD* si choisist lanel, *C* si coist lanel (-1)—606 *A* s. jusquel d., *B* s. jusquau d. menouel, *C* s. dusquen d. menuel, *D* s. jusques el cervel, *F* s. jusque el d. mamel, *G* s. dusqua d. meniel—607 *AB* Et jusquel p. li esfui (*B* effoi), *CG* Et dusqua (*G* au) p. li est fui (*G* li esfui), *D* Et jusques as piez est el vis—608 *AB* Nonques si ne sesvanui, *CG* Ne onques ne sesvanui, *D* Onques m.—609 *B* Ne de r. not si—610 *AB* f. li devint v.—611 *AB* Puis d., *C* Li d. la faice toute e. (+2), *G* Li d. t. espalie—612 *BF* Quesce f., *CG* Kesse (*G* Que esse +1) f., *D* f. el seinte marie—613 *ABCG* Ne voi je (*C* vo je) lanel, *D* La vo ie lennel, *F* Voi je dont lanel—614 *C* t. fuisse b.—615 *ABFG* Que jel vi, *D* vi hui main en

Cestui? Ce fis mon, or endroit! 616
Et por qoi l'a il ou mien mis?
Ja n'est il mie mes amis
Et si pens je qu'il le cuide estre.
Or est il, par Deu, plus que mestre 620
De cest art, ne sai qui l'aprist.
Diex! Comment est ce qu'il me mist?
A ce que je sui si soutise
Que je ne m'en sui garde prise 624
De l'anel qu'il m'a ou doi mis,
Or dira que c'est mes amis;
Ce fera mon, je n'en dout mie.
Dira il voir? Sui je s'amie? 628
Nenil! Por noient le diroit!
Ainz li manderé or endroit
Que il viengne parler a mi
S'il veut que le tiengne a ami, 632
Si li dirai qu'il le repraingne.
Je ne cuit pas qu'il en mespraingne
Vers moi, s'il ne velt que jou hace."
Atant commande c'on li face 636
58d Venir un vallet tout monté.
Ses puceles l'ont tant hasté

---

616 *ABCG* Ce fis mon fet (*C* mont dist) ele et que doit, *DF* m. et que doit
—617 *ABDF* Et (*F* Ne) p. q. la il el m., *C* Pour q. la il mis el mien (-1),
*G* p. cui lai jou ou—618 *D* Dont nest—619 *CG* si pense quil, *F* Si cuit je bien
quil—620 *C* par foi p., *F* Moult a este a sage m.—621 *C* q. aprist, *F* Et si
ne sai je q.—622 *ABDF* Et (*F* Mais) c. vint (*DF* fu) ce quil me prist (*B*
mesprist), *C* D. con fuisse ensi quil li m., *G* D. c. fusse quil—623 *AB* je ere
(*B* jere -1) si prise, *CF* je fui si souprisse, *DG* ge sui si sorprise—624 *BG om.*—
625 *B* lanel que ma, *G* lanel qui ma—626 *ABCDFG* quil est (*C* ert) m.—
627-628 *ABCFG* Dira (*G* Dirai) il voir sui je samie Nenil quar ce seroit
folie (*F* Ensi dira je nen dout mie)—629 *ABG* Certes por, *C* Certes ce seroit
por noient, *F* Mais p. n. voir le d.—630 *CG* A. li (*G* le) couvera ore e.—
631-632 *F om.*—632 *AD* que jel t., *G* Si wet q.—633 *B* d. qui le r., *F* Si le
d.—634 *CG* p. que il m., *D* c. que il en—636 *C* A. commanda con, *F* Elle
c.—638 *D* Les p. lont tost h., *G* Ces p.

Qu'il li est venuz tout montez.
"Amis, dist ele, or tost hurtez,                              640
Poingniez aprés le chevalier!
Dites li, si comme il a chier
M'amor, qu'il ne voist en avant,
Mes viengne arrere maintenant                                644
Parler a moi d'un sien afere."
--"Dame, fet il, je quit bien fere
Vostre volenté dusqu'en son."
Atant s'em part a esperon                                     648
Aprés le chevalier poingnant,
Cui Amors aloit destraingnant
De cele qui l'envoie querre.
En mains d'une liue de terre                                  652
L'a il ataint et retorné.
Sachiez qu'il se tint a buer né

De ce c'on l'avoit remandé;
Il n'a pas le mes demandé                                     656
Por qoi on remandé l'avoit:
Li aneaus qu'ele avoit ou doit
Ert l'achoison du remander.

---

639 *ABD* Quil i e., *CFG* Que chius (*FG* cil) e.—640 *AB* A. fet e, *C* t. montes,
*D* Vallet fait e. t. alez, *F* Frere fait e., *G* t. hates—641 *F* a. ce c., *G* a. c. (-1)
—644 *F* a. tout errant—645 *ABCD* m. de son a., *G* P. arriere de son a. (+1)—
646 *CG* D. dist il (*G* fait -1) bien le quit f.—647 *AB* V. message dusquen (*B*
jusquen) s., *C* v. dusqua sont, *D* V. voloir de chief en s., *F* v. jusque a s.—
648 *C* a espron (-1), *F* A. sen torne a, *G* A. se part—649 *C* c. errant, *D*
Enpres le—650 *ABDF* Qui a. (*F* lamours) a.—651 *AB* Por celi q., *CG* De
celi q. lenvoie q. Et qui le destraint molt et serre Li escuiers par aramanie
(*G* laramie), *F* Por celui q.—652 *CG* Dedens une lieue et demie, *F* A m.—
654 *CG* s. cor se tient a bon ne, *F* quil sen tient a bon ne—655 *CG* De chou
quele le remanda, *D* De cele quil lot r.—656 *ABF* Mes na p. au m., *CG* Mais
pas au m. ne demanda, *D* p. au m.—657 *B* q. len demande lavoit, *CG* q. on
lavoit remande, *D* q. remande on lavoit, *F* Sil set pourquoi le remandoit—
658 *B* quele ou doit avoit, *CG* Tost le savra par verite Li aniaus quele
avoit el doit Plus li grevoit que riens qui soit—659 *CG* Cert loccoisons del
r., *D* de r.

Ce li fist son oirre amender 660
Qu'il tarde cele qu'el le voie.
Li escuiers s'est en la voie
Du retor a lui acointiez;
He Diex! comme il fust ore liez 664
Du retorner, se por ce non
Qu'il estoit en g[ra]nt soupeçon
Qu'el ne li veille l'anel rendre.
Il dit qu'il s'iroit ainçois rendre 668
A Citiaus qu'il le represist.
"Ne cuit pas qu'ele mespresist,
Fet il, envers moi de cele oevre."
La joie du retor li cuevre 672
Le penser dont il ert en doute.
[Il est venuz a tant de route]
Comme il ot vers la forterece.
La dame, qui en grant destrece 676
Estoit et sor li desfendant,
59a      Ist de la sale descendant
Pas por pas aval le degré.

---

674 *om.*

---

660 *C* li fait s. o. aprester, *D* li fait s.—661 *ABCG* Quar tart (*G* tant) li est
quil le (*C* la) revoie, *D* Quil li est tart que il le, *F* Quil li est moult tart—
662 *BCG* e. est en—663-664 *G om.*—663 *ACD* de lui a., *B* a li a.—664
*ABCD* il en par fu l., *F* Il ne fu onques mais si l.—665 *CG* Del retour se p.
iche n., *F* De voiage se—666 *D* Que il e. en s., *F* Quil est en moult g.—
667-668 *CG om.*—667 *AB* Con ne li v. (*B* voussist) lanel, *D* Quele li v.,
*F* Que nel remant pour anel—668 *B* siroit avant r., *F* Mes si dist quil siroit
ains r.—669 *AB* cistiaus, *CG* De laniel quil le (*G* nel) r., *D* citeax, *F* citiaux
—670 *B* Ne quist p., *CG* p. quil (*G* kele) entrepresist, *DF* quel en m.—671
*ABCG* Envers moi f. (*CG* dist) il de tele (*C* cele) o., *D* de cest o., *F* il vers
moi dune tele o.—672 *F* li oeuvre—673 *AB* Le pensse d. il est en, *C* le pensee
d. il se d., *G* Le grant pensee d. il se d. (+1) Que je ne men sui garde prise—
675 *C* Com il est v., *D* Quanquil pot envers la fortrece—676 *CD* q. a g.—677
*ABCG* E. seur (*C* sous) son cors d., *D* E. envers lui d.—678 *CDG* s. maintenant, *F* s. en d.—679 *CDG* a. les degres, *F* a. un d.

Porpenseement et de gre                                680
Vient en la cort por l'i deduire;
L'anelet voit en son doit luire,
Qu'ele veut rendre au chevalier.
"S'il m'en fet ja point de dangier,                    684
Fet ele, et il nu velt reprandre,
Por ce ne l'iré je pas prandre
Par ses biaus cheveus.  Se je puis,
Ainz le menré desor ce puis,                           688
Si parlerai illec a lui;
S'il nu velt prandre sanz anui,
Je rompré molt tost la parole,
Comment?  Je n'iere pas si fole                         692
Que je le giete en mi la voie.
Ou dont?  En tel leu c'on nel voie,
Ce ert ou puis, n'est pas mençonge;
Ja puis n'en ert ne que de songe                       696
Chose dite qui me messiece.
Dont n'ai ge ore esté grant piece
O mon seignor sanz vilanie?

---

686 ni li lere je pas p. (+1)

---

680 *B* pourpenseement et (-1), *F A* penseement et—681 *AB* Vint en, *CG*
Vint (*G* Vient) en la c. p. soi d., *D* p. moi d., *F* Ala en la c. por d.—682 *AB*
En son doit vit lanelet l., *CG* Laniel v. (*C* vit) en s. d. reluire—683 *DF* Quele
doit r.—684 *C* Se il men f. p., *G* f. jai (*sic*) p.—685 *C* nu reveut r. (+1),
*G* Dist e.—686 *G* nel li lairai pas—687 *D* p. cez beax c.—688 *AB* m. ja sor
cel p., *C* m. la se jou puis, *D* A. len m. ja s. cel p., *FG* A. len m.—690 *AB* Sil
le v., *F* Et sil nel reprent s.—691 *AB* Je (*B* Jen) ronperai ci la, *CG* Jou
enprendrai (*C* emprenderai +1) ja la, *D* Ja nen repranrai la, *F* Tost len
reprenrai sa p.—692 *DG* niere ja si, *F* Ne ja de ce niere si—693 *CG* je li (*G*
le) meche e., *F* Que jete puer en—694 *AB* Mes en t. l. con ne le v., *CG*
Ne en t. l. ou (*G* que) on le v.—695 *CG* Ou dont el p. nest (*G* nes) p., *D*
Ert ce ou, *F* Droit en cel p. nert p.—696 *AB* e. plus que dun s., *CG* Ja plus
nen iert nes q. dun s., *D* Puis ne men e. ne q. dun s., *F* q. dun s.—697 *CDG*
me dessieche—698 *D* En ai je, *F* D. mar avrai e. tel p.—699 *F* [S] i longue-
ment sans druerie

Se cist par sa chevalerie 700
Et par soupirer devant mi
Veut ja que ju tiengne a ami
A cest premerain parlement,
Il avroit ançois durement 704
Deservi, se ju devoie estre."
Atant est cil entrez en l'estre,
Qui de tot ce ne se prent garde;
Il voit cele que molt esgarde 708
Volentiers aler par la cort.
Il descent lués et vers li cort,
Si con chevaliers fet vers dame.
Si dui conpaingnon ne nule ame 712
De l'ostel ne li font anui.
Fet il: "Bone aventure ait hui,
Ma dame, a qui je sui et iere."
Ne l'a or en autre maniere 716
Ferue du poing lez l'oïe.
59*b*    Ele a hui mainte chose oïe
Qui molt li touche pres du cuer.
"Sire, fet ele, alons la fuer 720
Seoir sor ce puis por deduire."
Or n'est il riens qui li puist nuire,
Ce dit, puis qu'el l'aqueut si bel;

---

700 *D* Se cil p., *F* . . . nt cil p.—701 *ABCFG* Ou p.—702 *B* ja quel t. (-1),
*F* V. que je le t.—703 *D* A cel p., *G* p. parlent (-1)—704 *A* Il lavroit, *B* a.
a touz d., *D* Il i avra ainz d., *F* Il lavroit a. autrement, *G* a. mout d. (+1)—
705 *D* D. que il le doie e., *F* D. sil le devoit e.—706 *C* e. chius e., *G* en li
e. (+1)—708 *A* v. celi q., *BCG* v. celi qui m. lesgarde, *D* Ainz v. celui q.,
*F* Et v. celi q. il e.—710 *D* d. lors et, *F* l. contre lui c.—711 *F* c. chevalier
font v.—712 *AB* c. nont nule asme, *CG* ne nul autre a.—713 *AB* De loster
ne, *F* De laiens ne—714 *AB* A foi b., *CG* Che (*G* Cil) dist b.—715 *ABG* a
cui je—716 *CG* Ne ma or, *F* Ne lai hui en—717 *CG* Feru du p. deles (*G*
dales) loie—718 *F* h. tante c., *G* Quele a m. (-1)—719 *B* li touchent p.,
*C* t. poi au c., *DF* m. poi li touchent au c., *G* li torne poi au c.—720 *ABCG*
S. dist e., *D* a. ca fuer—721 *ABCG* S. cel p., *F* S. lez ce—722 *AB* Il nest
chose q., *C* r. quil li—723 *ABCFG* p. que laqueut, *D* d. ele puis laqueut bel

Or cuide bien par son anel                    724
Avoir et s'amor et sa grace.
Mes n'est encor preu en la trace
Por qoi il se doive esjoïr;
Ainz qu'il peüst lez li seïr,                  728
Ot il chose qui li desplet.
"Sire, fet ele, s'il vos plet,
Dites moi, la vostre merci,
C'est vostre anel que je tien ci,              732
Por qoi le me donnastes ore?"
–"Douce dame, fet il, encore,
Quant m'en irai, si l'avrez vos;
Si vos dirai, ce sachiez vos,                  736
Si nel tenez pas a faintié,
De tant vaut il miex la moitié
Qu'il a en vostre doit esté.
S'il vos plesoit, en cest esté                 740
Le savroient mi anemi,
Se vos m'aviëz a ami

---

726 Il nest

---

724 *ABCDFG* Bien (*F* Tout) c. avoir p.–725 *ABCDG* Conquise samor et sa g. (*C* lamor et la g.), *F* Recouvre samor et sa gra . . . –726 *AB* Il nest e. (*B* ancore +1) p. en la nasse, *CG* M. il nen est pas bien aisse (*G* en nasse), *D* la nasse, *F* M. il nest pas encore a ce–727 *A* se doie e., *B* se doit e., *C* P. quil se doie resjoir, *D* q. se (-1), *F* Quil se doie esjoir ensi, *G* P. quil se doie esjoir (-1)–728 *CG* Puis quil (*G* que il) pot (-1), *F* Quil a moult poi sis delez li–729 *CG* Not il, *F* Quant il oy tout autre plait–730 *CG* S. dist e., *D* Dame f. il et que v.–731 *D* Dirai le vos v., *F* Quar me dites par vo m.–732 *ABCDG* je voi ci–733 *ABD* me lessastes o., *F* le lessastes vous o.–734 *F* En mon doit si ferai je encore, *G* d. dist il–735 *C* Q. je men i. laveres v. (+1), *D* men ira si, *F* Se dieu plaist quant je men irai, *G* Q. je me i.–736 *AB* Je v., *CG* Je le vous doins ce, *D* Gel v. dorrai tot a estrox, *F* Dame fet il si vous dirai–737 *C* Sel ne t. p. a faintise, *D* Nel t. a point de f., *F* Mais n., *G* t. a f. (-1)–738 *B* m. de la (+1)–740 *CG* p. a c.–741 *C* Le saveroient mi (+1)–742 *CG* Que v. maiies (*G* maves) a vostre a., *D* v. me tenez a

Reçut, et je vos a amie."
--"En non Dieu, ce n'i a il mie,                         744
Fet ele, ançois i a tot el!
Ja puis n'istré de cest ostel,
Si m'aït Dex, se morte non,
Que vos avroiz ne cri ne non                             748
De m'amor, por rien que je voie.
Vos n'en estes pas en la voie,
Ainz en estes molt forvoiez!
Tenez, je veil que vos l'aiez,                           752
Vostre anel, que je n'en voil mie.
Ja mar me tenrez a amie
Por garde que j'en aie fete."
Or se despoire, or se deshete                            756
Cil qui cuidoit avoir tot pris.

59c     Fet il: "Mains en vaudroit mes pris,
Se c'est a certes que je voi.
Onques mes nule joie n'oi                                760
Qui si tost me tornast a ire."
--"Comment donques, fet ele, sire,
Avez i vos anui ne honte
De moi, a qui noient ne monte                            764

---

759 Se cert a

---

743 *D* Et ge vos avoie a a.—744 *D* ce ne vueil ge m., *F* E non—745 *CG* F.
(*G* Dist) e. ains i avera (*G* ara) t. (+1), *D* Sire fist ele ainz i a el—746 *D* p.
nistrez de—747 *F* Ce sachiez bien se—748 *ABDF* v. avrez ne, *C* Ken aiies
lotroi ne le don, *G* Que naies se lotroi non (-1)—749 *B* q. gi v.—750 *ABDF*
e. preu en, *C* e. mie en—752 *AB* v. aiez—753 *ABF* que (*F* quar) je nen ruis
m.—754 *ABG* m. men t.—755 *CD* je en (+1), *G* P. garder ke j. a. afaire—
756 *G* se deporte or—758 *ABCG* Mains (*B* Mes) en voudroit fait il m. (*CG*
vos) p., *D* Mielz en v. fait mon p. (-1), *F* Moult en v. ja mieux mes p.—759
*ABD* je oi, *F* Fait il se cestoit voirs que joi—762 *C* G. fait ele donques s.,
*F* C. fet elle biaux douz s., *G* d. dist e.—763 *AB* i donc a., *CG* A. vous donc
a., *D* A. en vos a., *F* Vous ni avez a.—764 *ACG* a cui n. ne (*G* nen) m.

Vers vos d'amor ne de lingnage?
Je ne faz mie grant outrage
Se ge vos voil vostre anel rendre;
Il n'i a, voir, fors du reprandre,                    768
Car je n'ai droit ou retenir,
Puis que je ne vos voil tenir
A ami, car je mesferoie."
--"Diex, fet il, se ge me feroie                      772
D'un coutel tres parmi la cuisse,
Ne me feroie tele angoisse
Comme ces paroles me font.
Mal fet qui destruit et confont                       776
Ce dont on puet estre au deseure;
Trop me cort force d'amor seure
Por vos, et met en grant destrece,
Ne ja mar baeroit a ce                                780
Nule du mont que jel repreingne.
Ja puis, a foi, Dex ne me praigne
A bone fin que jel prendrai,

---

780 m. baerez a

---

765 *C* Damours vers vous ne, *D* ne l. (-1), *F* A vous davoir ne—766 *CG* g. hontaige, *D* g. ostraige—767 *G* je ne wel v. a prendre—768 *ABCFG* Il le vous covient a r. (*C* covient r. -1)—769 *ABC* d. au r., *DFG* d. el r.—770 *CF* que ne v. v. retenir, *D* Des que ge nel vueil deservir—771 *D* Quar bien sai que ge m., *F* a. je en m.—772 *C* fait se (-1)—773 *A* p. les cuisses, *B* c. p. les cuisses (-1), *F* Ja dun c., *G* c. tout p.—774 *AB* f. teus (*B* tel) anguisses, *CG* Ne soufferoie je tant (*G* s. t.) dangoisse (+1), *F* me feroit il t.—775 *CG* p. ci font—777 *AB* Chose d. len est au d., *CFG* d. il p. e. au (*G* el) d.—778 *A* T. mi c., *C* Forche damor me keurt trop s., *F* T. durment me queurt amor s.—779 *B* et mest en, *D* P. voir mestuet en—780 *AB* Chose nest qui a ce me mece, *CG* Car nest cose qui vous conteche, *D* Ja m. baerois en destrece, *F* a ceste—781 *CG* Que je nel (*G* ne) faice ains que je (*G* jel) prengne, *D* N. de moi q., *F* Por riens du m. q. je le prengne—782 *ABCG* Ja diex a f. puis ne, *F* Jaim miex que male mort me—783 *B* f. quel j., *C* f. quant je le prenderai (+2), *D* f. quant gel, *F* Au jour que je le reprendrai

Ainz l'avrez et si vos lerai 784
Mon cuer avec en vo servise,
Qu'il n'est riens qui a vo devise
Vos serve si bien ne si bel
Comme entre mon cuer et l'anel." 788
Fet ele: "N'en parlez vos onques,
Car vos en perdrïez adonques
M'acointance et ma seürté,
Se vos outre ma volenté 792
Me volez fere a vos m'esprendre.
Il le vos covient a reprendre!"
--"Non fet."--"Si fet. La n'a que dire,
Ou vos estes molt plus que sire, 796
Se vostre anuis a ce m'esforce
59d Que vos le me voilliez par force
Maugré mien fere retenir.
Tenez!"--"Ja mes nu quier tenir." 800
--"Si ferez."--"Je non ferai voir."
--"Volez le me vos fere avoir
A force?"--"Nenil voir, amie.

---

795 Si fet non fet

---

784 *AB* Mes vous lavrez et si avrai, *CG* Mais vous lares et vous donrai, *D* Mais vos larez et ge larai, *F* et je lairai—785 *CG* a. a vo, *D* c. avez vos de s.—786 *ABCG* Nil nest, *D* Si nest r. q. a vos d.—787 *CDFG* b. et si—789 *C* Elle dist nen p. v. donques, *F* Elle li dist nen p. o., *G* Elle dist nen—790 *ABCFG* perderiez—791 *A* ma feaute, *B* ma seulte, *D* et mafinite, *F* et mamiste (-1)—792 *ABCDG* vos contre ma—793 *AB* Me voliez f. a v. entendre, *CG* Me faisies ja vo (*G* vostre) anel prendre, *DF* Volez ore (*F* donques) vers moi m.—795 *CG* f. chi na, *DF* f. ni a q.—796 *F* Dont seriez vous m., *G* Or estes vous m.—797 *B* ce menforce, *CG* se vos aniaus a, *F* vos a. a—798 *ABFG* a force, *D* me laissiez a f.—799 *B* M. mi f., *D* Ne malgre mon cuer r.—800 *F* Dame ja, *G* m. nel q. ja mais t.—801 *D* Ja si f. non—802 *C* Voleme vous f. (-1), *F* le vous moi f.—803 *AB* f naje, *CF* f. naje douche a., *D* f. naje v., *F* Sor mon pois naie douce a., *G* f. naje v. douce a. (+1)

Bien sai ce pooir n'ai ge mie,                       804
Ce poise moi, si m'aït Diex!
Ja puis vilenie ne dues
Ne m'avenroit, c'est ma creance,
Se vos en un poi d'esperance          808
Me metïez por conforter."
—"Ausi bien porrïez hurter
A ce perron le vostre chief
[Que vos en venissiez a chief];          812
Si lou que vos le repreingniez."
—"Il m'est vis que vos m'apreingniez,
Fet il, a chanter de Renart;
Je me leroie ainz une hart          816
Lacier ou col que jel preïsse.
Ne sai que je vos en feïsse
Lonc plet qu'au reprandre n'a rien."
—"Sire, fet ele, or voi je bien          820
Que ce vos fet fere enresdie,
Quant parole que je vos die
Ne vos puet au prandre mener.
Or vos veil je aconjurer,          824

---

812 *om.*—822 Que por parole que je d.

---

804 *AB* s. tel p., *CG* s. que tel p. nai (*G* nai jou +1) m., *D* s. la force navez
m., *F* E non dieu ce ni a il m.—806 *F* Ja mais v.—807 *D* Ne mavenrra c.—
809 *ACG* p. reconforter, *BD* Me metez p. reconforter—810 *ABCDFG*
Vous porriez (*B* porrez, *D* poez) ausi bien h.—811 *AB* A cel p., *CG* A
cest p.—812 *CG om.*, *B* Vous an v. ja a, *D* Quar v. en venriez a, *F* Quen
peussiez venir a—813 *CG om.*, *D* Si vueil q., *F* Si vous lo que le—814
*ABCDG* Il (*G* Or) sanble que, *F* Ha dame mais vous estaigniez—815 *ABCDG*
F. il (*CG* Dist elle) a c. de bernart, *F* La dolour qui mesprent et art—816
*CDFG* Ainz me l. a u.—817 *A* Poncier el c. quel repreisse, *B* L. el c. quel
repreisse, *C* Pendre mon c. quel repressise, *F* Rompre le c. quel repreisse,
*G* Prendre mon c. q.—818 *C* q. plus v. en desisse, *F* s. pour quoi je v. f., *G*
en dessisse—819 *AB* p. au r., *CG* quau r. na nient, *F* p. quel r.—821 *B* f.
enresderie (+1), *G* ce fait f. (-1)—822 *CG* car p.—823 *C* p. amener—824 *C*
Premiers v. v. a., *D* Mais or v. v. ge conjurer, *F* v. en v. je conjurer, *G* Proiier
v. v. et conjurer

Par la grant foi que me devez,
Et proier que le reprenez,
Si chier con vos avez m'amor."
Or n'i a il, en Dieu amor,        828
Tor c'un seul: qu'il ne li coviengne
A reprendre, ou qu'el[e] nu tiengne
A desloial ou a jengleus.
"Diex, fet il, li qex de ces geus        832
Partiz m'est or li mains mauvais?
Or sai je bien, se ge li lais,
Ele dira je ne l'aim mie.
Qui tant estraint croste que mie        836
En saut, ce par est trop estraint.
Cis sairemenz m'a si ataint
61*a*    Que li lessiers ne m'i est preuz,
Ançois cuit je que li miens preuz        840
Et m'onors i soit au reprandre,
Se je ne voil de molt mesprandre
Vers ma gentil dame anoree,

---

830 ou quel nu (-1)

---

825 *ABC* P. cele f. q. moi d., *D* Que sor la f., *F* La g. f. q. vous me, *G* P. le f. ke vous moi d.—826 *ABCG* Vous proi q. vous le, *D* Vos pri je q. vous le prenez, *F* q. vous le prenez—827-828 *F. om.*—827 *CG* chier que v.— 828 *AB* en ceste error, *D* d. enmor—829 *B* s. qui ne, *C* Tout cun, *F* Or ni a plus quil ne c.—830 *C* ou quil nu (-1), *D* R. que quil en aviegne, *F* R. ou quele ne le t., *G* A prendre u quele le t.—831 *AB* d. et a, *CG* A (*G* Con) d. et anieus, *D* Sil le retient il est gengleus—832 *ABDF* ces (*D* ce) deus, *G* He d. dist il li q. des deus—833 *ABCG* Mest or partis li, *D* Mest au partir li, *F* Mest ore m.—834 *CD* je le l., *F* Or voi je—835 *ABF* Quele d., *CG* Quele d. (*G* dirai) que nen ainc m.—836 *D* Q. plus e.—837 *AB* ce est par grant destroit, *C* Ensault certes trop est destrois, *D* t. destraint, *F* ce qui est plus estroit, *G* En vole cest par t. destroit—838 *ABG* si destroit, *C* s. mest si destrois, *D* s. est trop estraint, *F* Je le voi bien au grant destroit—840 *C* A. quide q., *F* A. voi bien que mes grans p., *G* A. cui jou—841 *CG* Et mes pourfis s., *D* monors si s. el r., *F* monors si est—842 *D* v. auques mesprandre, *F* v. forment mesprandre—843 *ABCG* ma douce d.

Qui s'amor m'a aconjuree,                              844
Et la grant foi que je li doi.
Quant je l'avrai mis en mon doi,
Si ert il siens, la ou il iert;
Se ge faz ce qu'ele me quiert,                         848
Je n'i puis avoir s'enor non.
N'est pas amis qui jusqu'en son
Ne fet au voloir de s'amie,
Et sachiez que cil n'aimme mie                         852
Qui riens qu'il puisse en lait a fere.
Si doi atorner mon afere
Du tot en son commandement
Car il n'en doit estre autrement                       856
S'a la seue volenté non."
Il na noma pas par son non
Quant il dit: "Dame, jel prendrai
Par un covent: que j'en ferai                          860
Aprés la vostre volenté
La moie, encor ait il esté
En ce doit que je voi si bel."
--"Et je vos rent donques l'anel                       864

---

859 dame jel p.

---

844 *CG* Q. de samor ma conjuree, *D* Q. si forment ma conjure, *F* samor
mi a conjuree—845 *D* Et sor la f.—846 *C* Que je lavra m., *F* La ou il est ens
en—847 *ABCG* Si sera il s. ou il (*CG* quil) i., *D* Sert il s. ja u ae nen ert
(*sic*), *F* Siert siens laniaux la—848 *D* ce quel me requiert—850 *AB* p. sages
q. dusquen s., *C* jusqua s., *F* N. mie a. q. jusque a s. (+1), *G* q. jusques a
s. (+1)—851 *ABCDFG* f. la volente samie—852 *CG* Molt est cil de mauvaise
vie, *F* S. ou il ne laime m.—853 *ABCD* quil puist en, *F* La ou point en
remaint a f., *G* Que r. quil puist ne l.—854 *AB* Je d., *CG* Ains doit a. son
a., *D* d. la doner m., *F* Je d. a. cest a.—855 *ABCFG* t. a s., *D* Descot a s.—
856 *ABCDG* il ne d., *F* Que ne d. pas e.—858 *AB* Il nel n., *CG* Il nen nouma
mie p. non, *D* Ne lapela p., *F* Ne la n.—859 *CG* Ains a d.—860 *ABF* P.
covent que je en f., *CG* P. couvenant ke jen f., *D* que ge dirai—861 *D* Enpres
la, *G* la moie v.—863 *ABCG* En cel d.—864 *C* Et je v. et je v. r. (+3), *D*
Donques vos ren ge vostre ennel, *F* Tenez et je vos rent lanel

Par covent que vos l'en faciez."
N'est enveilliz ne esfaciez
Li sens du vaillant chevalier;
Tot enprenant de cuer entier                       868
Le prist tot porpenseement,
Si le resgarde doucement.
Au reprandre dit: "Grant merciz!
Por ce n'est pas li ors nerciz,                    872
Fet il, s'il vient de vo biau doit!"
Cele s'en sozrist, qui cuidoit
Qu'il le deüst remetre el sien,
Mes il fist un plus greingnor sen                  876
Dont molt grant joie li vint puis:
Il s'est acoutez seur le puis,
61*b*    Qui n'estoit que toise et demie
Parfonz, si ne meschoisi mie                       880
De l'eaue, qui ert bele et clere,
L'ombre de la dame qui ere
La riens ou mont que plus amot.
"Sachiez, fet il tot a un mot,                      884

---

865 *C* c. en f., *DG* v. le f.—866 *AB* Nert enviesis ne, *C* Nestoit muisis ne
enfachies, *D* Nest pas devers moi enpiriez, *F* Nestoit enviezis nesfaciez,
*G* Nest il envoisies nenfaities—867-868 *D* inv.—867 *ABCDG* del gentil c.,
*F* Laniaux du courtois c.—868 *ABCG* T. esprendanz de, *D* Toz espris et cuer
et entier, *F* Moult joians et de—870 *C* Si lesgarda molt d., *D* le demande
d., *F* . . . le regarda d.—871 *F* r. et d.—873 *AB* de cel b., *CG* Dist il sil (*G*
si) v. de cel b., *D* Por ce quil v. de ce b., *F* de ce b.—874 *F* C. sousrit qui
bien quidoit, *G* C. ki sorist ki c.—875 *CG* Ke il le remesist el s., *D* Quele d.—
876 *AB* f. ainz un molt grant s., *C* il a fait un molt grant bien, *D* Ainz
fist apres un g., *F* il a fet un autre s., *G* il en fist un molt grant s.—877
*ABCG* Qua g. j. li torna p.—878 *F* Il est a.—879 *D* Qui navoit que—880
*CG* ne meschoisist m., *F* P. il ne—881-882 *CG* inv.—881 *A* Laigue q. e. et.
b., *B* Leaue q. e. (-1), *C* En laigue ki est b. et chere, *DFG* En leaue qui ert b.
—882 *C* Lombre a la d. ki bele e., *G* Lombre la d. ki la e.—883 *AB* r. el m.
q. miex a. (*B* amoit), *CDFG* r. el (*F* du) m. quil (*G* ki) p. a. (*CG* amoit)—
884 *F* Fet il lues droit t.

Que je n'en reporterai mie,
Ainz l'avra ja ma douce amie,
La riens que j'aing miex enprés vos."
--"Diex, fet ele, ci [n']a que nos;                            888
Ou l'avrez vos si tost trovee?"
--"En non Deu, ja vos ert mostree
La preuz, la gentil qui l'avra."
--"Ou est, en non Deu?"--"Vez la la,                           892
Vostre bel ombre qui l'atent."
L'anel a pris et si li tent.
"Tenez, fet il, ma douce amie!
Puis que ma dame n'en velt mie,                                896
Vos le prandrez bien sanz mellee."
L'eaue s'est un petit troblee
Au cheoir que li aneaus fist,
Et, quant li ombres se desfist:                                900
"Vez, dame, fet il, or l'a pris.
Molt en est amendez mes pris
Quant ce qui de vos est l'emporte.
Car n'eüst or ne huis ne porte                                 904
La jus! Si s'en venroit par ci
Por dire la seue merci
De l'oneur que fete m'en a."

---

888 ci a q.

---

885 *A* nen reprenderai m., *BCG* ne le retenrai m., *F* Je ne len r.—886 *AF* A. lavera ma, *B* A. lavra ma (-1), *CG* lavra ma tres de., *D* lavra ma dame mamie —887 *ABF* jaim plus apres v., *CG* q. plus aim apres v.—888 *G* dist e. ci na ke vous—889 *B* Ou lavez v., *D* t. trove, *G* ou aves v.—890 *AB* Par mon chief tost v.,   *F* Moult par tans v. sera m.—892 *AC* V le,   *F* e. par mon chief v. le la, *G* U est ele diex vees le la (+1)—893 *D* Vit le b., *G* b. lombre—894 *ABD* Lanelet prent et vers (*D* il) li t., *CG* Laniel li rue et il le prent, *F* Il prent lanelet si li t.—895 *F* Prendez le f. il bele a.—897 *C* le prendes b.— 898 *ABCG* Laigue sest, *D* Leve sest, *F* Liaue sest—900 *F* o. sen d.—901 *ABCG* V. fet il dame or, *G* or a p.—902 *CG* Bien en e. a. vos p.—903 *D* Quar ce q. de v. ert lemporte, *F* ce que de, *G* qui est de v. lemporte—904 *A* neust il ore h., *BD* neust ore h., *F* neust il ne h.—907 *C* loneur quele faite ma

He, Diex! Si buer i asena 908
A cele cortoisie fere,
C'onques mes riens de son afere
Ne fu a la dame plesans.
Toz reverdis et esprenans 912
Li a geté ses euls es siens:
Molt vient a homme de grant sens
Qui fet cortoisie au besoing.
"Orainz ert de m'amor si loing 916
Cil hom, et or en est si pres!
Onques mes devant ne aprés
61c N'avint, puis qu'Adanz mort la pome,
Si bele cortoisie a home; 920
Ne sai comment il l'en membra.
Quant por m'amor a mon ombre a
Jeté son anel enz ou puis,
Or ne li doi je ne ne puis 924
Plus veer le don de m'amor;
Ne sai por quoi je li demor,
C'onques hom si bien ne si bel
Ne conquist amor par anel, 928

---

919 que a. (+1)

---

908 *A* si buen i, *BD* si bien i, *CG* com bien (*G* boin) i, *F* d. tant bon i—
909 *C* c. a f.—910 *ABF* Onques m., *CG* Nonques m.—911 *C* fu la d. ossi
p.—912 *CG* T. embrases (*G* embramis) et alumans, *D* T. revestuz et apre-
nanz, *F* Entalentis et—913 *AFG* e. es s., *B* Li a ces iaux getez es, *C* e. as s.,
*D* e. elz s.—914 *D* M. muet a, *G om.*—915 *A* Quil f., *D* Et dit la dame par b.
—916 *B* ert mamor (-1), *C* O. estoit cius hom si l., *F* Fet elle orains iert
cis si, *G* O. en estoit chius si—917 *A* Cis h., *CDG* Qui (*D* Et) orendroit
estoit (*DG* en est) si, *F* De mamor or—918 *D* m. orainz ne a., *FG* Conques
m.—919 *F* que a. (+1), *B* manja (+1)—921 *D* il avenra—922 *B* a monbre a
(-1), *D* Quar p. lamor a—923 *ABG* e. el p., *C* a. en son p., *D* a. en cest p.,
*F* cel a. en ce p.—924 *C* Comment donques veer li p., *F* ne le d., *G* Or nest
il drois ne ne p. (-1)—925 *C* Le don ne lotroi de, *D* Devaer le d.—926 *D* li
devor, *F* je le d.—927 *ABD* Onques h., *C* Nonques h.—928 *D* c. dame p.

Ne miex ne doit avoir amie."
Sachiez qu'ele nu bleça mie,
Quant ele dit: "Biaus douz amis,
Tot vostre cuer ont el mien mis                     932
Cil doz mot et cil plesant fet,
Et li dons que vos avez fet
A mon ombre en l'onor de moi;
Or metez le mien en vo doi:                         936
Tenez! Je vos doing comme amie.
Je cuit que vos ne l'avrez mie
Mains du vostre, encor soit il pire."
--"De l'onor, fet il, de l'Empire                   940
Ne me fesist on pas si lié."
Molt se sont andui envoisié
Sor le puis de tant comme il peurent.
Des besiers dont il s'entrepeurent                  944
Va chascun la douçor au cuer.
Lor bel oel n'en gietent pas puer
La parole, ce est du mains.

---

938 c. vos ne lamerez m.

---

929 *AB* ne dut a., *D* Nus ne d. a. mielz a., *F* Ne si bien doie a., *G* Que m.
deust a.—930 *ADG* quele nen b., *B* quele ne b., *C* quele nel b., *F* S. quel ne
le blece m.—932 *ABF* Tout ont mon c. el vostre m., *C* T. ai en vous le mien
cuer m., *D* T. ont vostre c. el, *G* T. ai mon c. el vostre m.—933 *ABD* C. (*A*
Cist) d. m. et li p., *F* C. plesant mot et c. bien f.—934 *CG* v. maves f., *D*
li dels q.—935 *G* A monbre (-1)—936 *D* Metez le m. en vostre d., *F* Or
tenez metez en—937 *ABCDG* T. jel v., *F* Le mien jel v.—938 *ABF* c. vos ne
lamerez m., *C* Je cuide v. nel haires m., *D* Ge croi v. ne lamerez m., *G* Je
croi que v. nen hares m.—940 *B om.*, *F* De toute lonor de, *G* lonor dist
il—941 *B* f. len p., *C* f. nus hon si, *D* me feisse pas si, *F* Je cuit nel f. on si,
*G* on hui si—942 *F* M. sont puis a.—943-944 *G om.*—944 *C* De baisier car
faire le dorent, *D* b. tant com il lor plorent—945 *C* A c. le don cuer a c.,
*G* Et fist c. don cuer a c.—946 *ABC* o. ne g., *D* Lor amor ne g., *F* o. nont
pas jete puer, *G* Des bials ne jetent p. (-2)—947 *ABD* Lor part ce est ore
del m., *CG* Lor partie cest or del (*G* ore des +1) m., *F* Lor part del deduit
cest du

De tel geu comme on fet des mains        948
Estoit ele dame et il mestre,
Fors de celui qui ne puet estre,
Dont il lor covendra molt bien.
N'i covient mes penser de rien        952
Jehan Renart a lor afere;
S'il a nule autre chose a fere,

---

948 *ABD* g. con len f., *CG* De ceus (*G* tel) g. c. on f. des rains, *F* De cel jeu—949 *C* et cis m., *D* et m. (-1), *F* De cert elle d.—950 *D* Mais du gieu que or ne, *F* F. du jeu q.—951 *ABCG* De celui lor c. b., *F* Des autres lor estut il b.—952-954 *F illegible at the end of each line*—952 *AB* m. baer de r., *CG* Nen c. ja p. de r., *D* Nen c. m. parler a., *F* Nen c. pas penser ... —953 *D* Mais aut chascuns a son a., *F* Ci le laira a lo ...
—953 *C continues:*   Car puis orent il molt boin tans
                   Et molt sentramerent tous tans
                   Ne vaurrai plus lonc conte faire
                   Jehans Renars a lor afaire
                   Sil a nule autre chose a faire
                   Il le fera sans nul contraire
                   Bien puet son penser metre aillors
     *CG end:*      Contes vous ki saves millors
                   Mout vient a home de grant sens (*C om.*)
                   Car de cestui (*G* cesti) plus ne dirai
                   Quant lieus en ert sen (*G* si) parlerai
                   De la boine vie kil orent
                   Quant boin lor fu et il lor plorent
                   En grant joie et (*G om.* -1) en grant deduit
                   Furent souvent et jor et (*G om.* -1) nuit
                   Et les (*G om.* -1) tournois souvent antoit (*G* hastoit)
                   Et lounour de tous en avoit
                   Bien le savoit sa douche amie
                   Ki molt en ert joians et lie
                   Car il estoit plaisans et dous (*G om.*)
                   Et se faisoit amer a tous (*G om.*)
954 *D* Se il a a., *F*?, *G* a n. c. a (-1)

Bien puet son penser metre aillors.
Que, puisque lor sens et Amors                              956
Ont mis andeus lor cuers ensemble,
Du geu qui remaint, ce me semble

61*d*   Venront il bien a chief andui.
Et or s'en taise atant mes hui;                           960
Ici fenist li Lais de l'Ombre,
Contez, vos qui savez de nombre.

-------------------

955 *AB* pensse
955 *F ends*:          Je puis bien ces lay ci fenir
                       Ci les lais andeus couvenir
                       Si metrai mon penser aillours
                       Quar puis que lor sens et amours
                       A mis lors cuers andeus ensamble
                       Du jeu qui remaint ce me samble
                       Verront il bien a chief andui
                       Or le lairai atant maishui
                                 Explicit
956 *AB* Puis que l. s. et lor a., *D* Quar p.—957 *AB* Et quil ont mis l.—
959 *D ends*:          Ne covient pas ci a parler
                       Ge vueil ci mon conte finer
                                 Explicit
960 *AB* or me tais a.

# COMMENTARY

*Title*: Every ms of the *Lai* indicates a title marked in a medieval hand. *ABCDEG* all agree, with only minor variation (see variants), on the use of the word *ombre*. Of those versions, *DG* also have *anel* as part of the title as does *F*, which alone of the mss mentions the *chevalier* and the *dame*, but does not use the word *ombre*. At line 52, all the mss but *F* have the title with the word *ombre* at the rhyme; the whole prologue ending with this line is missing in *F* which also lacks 961-962 where the title also figures in the other mss.

5. I have followed the lead of Orr and the reading of mss *ABCDG* in emending from *oiseus* to *garcon*. *Oiseus*, whose meaning 'idle' is not usually applied to those who destroy, could have been copied from line 3. For *garcon*, see Tobler-Lommatzsch s.v. *garcon* where this line is cited and the word is defined as pejorative, 'miserable, wretched (boy).'

8. The whole line, *Vilains est qui ses gas en fet*, appears twice consecutively in *E*, a result, surely, of a moment of inattention on the part of the scribe.

9. There has been some debate on the meaning of *s'aovre*. Bédier (1913) gives *aovrer*, refl. 's'employer,' quoted in Tobler-Lommatzsch s.v. *aovrer* where they cite this instance, among others. Limentani and Lecoy both agree. Orr and Levy, however, say that the infinitive is rather *aovrir*, 'to show oneself, be manifest.' It seems to me that the former assignment, that is, 'to put oneself to work,' is a better one: the image of Courtesy dedicating itself to writing is much more vivid than the passive one of Courtesy as manifest. There is nothing, however, in the morphology or syntax which precludes either reading.

14. With Orr I have emended from *fox* to *fel* according to *AB*. In this way it is possible to differentiate the *fox* of 13 who

is easily swayed from writing from the *fel* who does not respect what is written.

16-17.   'For I can no more make this finger as long as that one, I believe, than one could today make a lowly person courtly.'   To understand this image, compare the length of two fingers on the same hand; generally speaking, no two are of equal length.

21-24.   Guillaume and the *escoufle* ('kite,' a kind of hawk) refer to another of Jean Renart's poems, *Le Roman de l'escoufle*. As was stated in the Introduction (p. 12), the reference here has helped establish Jean Renart as author of that unsigned romance and to fix its relative date as preceding the composition of the *Lai*.

27.   Orr changes *parenz* to *avoir* following *ABCG* with a note to this line stating, "DE, disliking the repetition of *avoir*, write *parenz ne amis*, which suits the story of the *Escoufle*, but does not fit our context." I feel he is giving the word *parenz* too narrow an interpretation: it can imply wealth and nobility of birth as well as the existence of family members. Accordingly, I have retained the reading of *E, parenz*. On the non-elision of schwa /ə/ before a vowel (here *ne amis*) see M. Grammont, *Petit traité de versification française* (2ᵉ ed., Armand Colin, 1964, pp. 24-26) and Th. Elwert, *Traité de versification française des origines à nos jours* (Klincksieck, 1965, pp. 31-32), both of which discuss the optional character of the elision of schwa within a line of verse in Old French. Cf. lines 53, 355, 493, 525, 947.   For an opposite case, cf. 475 where reading *je entremetre* as a non-elision makes for a hypersyllabic line.

38.   On the meaning of the word *lai* see the Introduction, p. 8.   It is interesting to note that at line 50, at the rhyme, Jean Renart refers to his work as a *conte*, although he returns to *lai* in 52 and 961, both of which name the work as the *Lai de l'ombre*.

40-44.   For a discussion of *l'Eslit* and a probable attribution of the title to Miles de Nanteuil, see the Introduction, pp. 11-12.   Jean Renart's use of the verb *souploier* 'bow down before, render homage to' and the unusual syntax of 43, 'since the will has been chosen for me' seem to indicate that the poem was commissioned by the *Eslit*. No indication is given, however, as to whether the poet chose the subject matter himself. Noteworthy too (41-44) are the pairs of rhymes (*Eslit: delit, eslite: delite*) which are indicative of Jean Renart's pleasure in playing with language. Both to the ear and the eye, the pairs of rhymed words are very similar, but still count as different because of the final *e* and its effect on the pronunciation and appearance of the second pair. See notes to 46-49 and 962, and Introduction, p. 15.

46-49. The interpretation of these lines and especially of 48 (*Fox est se a la mer estrive*) is rather difficult. Jean Renart is comparing the writer to a navigator and saying that, at the successful completion of a sea voyage or a composition (note the pun on *rimer/ramer* in 46) both are esteemed by kings and counts. Orr, in an ingenious emendation to the text of *E*, added the line from *A* (*Qui a port de bien dire arrive*) as 48a, after ending 48 with a period, thereby indicating that if one arrives safely in port, one is crazy to struggle further against the sea. Then, whoever does manage to arrive at the port of good speech is better esteemed. I do not believe that the additional line is necessary, since 47 (*Que de haute mer vient a rive*) is sufficient reference for the *l'* of 49. For a further discussion of Orr's argument, see his "Textual Problems of the Lai de l'ombre" in *Studies (for) R. L. Graeme Ritchie* (Cambridge, 1949), pp. 137-146, O. Schultz-Gora, *Archiv* 157 (1930), 50 and P. Fay's review of Orr's edition, *RPh*, 2 (1949-1950), 340. On the comparison of navigator and poet, see E.-R. Curtius, *Europäische Literatur und lateinisches Mittelalter* (Bern, 1948), pp. 136-138.

54-55. The geographic setting is very vaguely specified in the text, somewhere on the border (*marche*) of the Empire in what is now eastern France and western Germany. Such vagueness is not surprising in a text where even the protagonists are unnamed. See Introduction, p. 10 and note to 59-64.

57. *Perchois* has been identified as Perthois, the general region in which the town of Perthes is located; that is, the department of the Haute-Marne. As Lejeune (*Jean Renart*, p. 259) points out, the region extends east of the Marne, there-

fore on the border of the Empire (see note to 54-55). Lecoy, who also accepts this identification of *Perchois* (edition, note to this line), remarks that the distance from Chaalons (sur-Marne) to Perthes is not great; Jean Renart is being ironic about the wide-spread reputation of his hero.

59-64.  M. P. Simonelli ("I giuochi semantico-compositivi del 'Lai de l'ombre' e un crittogramma di Jean Renart," *CN*, 35 (1975), p. 37) has suggested that the nameless hero is Loth, father of Gawain, and that his identity is hidden in the final words of these lines: *cil ot, Loth, dison, nom en ot, l'ot.* I agree with Lecoy (edition, note to the lines) that such an identification is unlikely, especially in view of good stylistic reasons for not assigning names to the protagonists; see the Introduction, p. 10 and note to 54-55. The syntax of the phrase *fil Lot* is not uncommon in Old French where an unambiguous genitive expression is frequently found without the preposition *de*; cf. Ménard, §4.

74-77.  "No maid nor lady ever heard of him without esteeming him greatly, nor was he ever strongly attracted to anyone without it going well for him. . . ." That is, women always responded to his interest, for how could they resist him? As Lecoy points out (edition, note to these lines) contrary to Limentani (note to 112-123), Jean Renart never says that the knight has never played at flirtation, but rather that he has never taken love seriously. For the omission of the first part of a compound preposition, in 75 and 77 where I have understood 'sans que,' see Ménard, §199a. Cf. 220, 264, 574, 661 and the Glossary s.v. *que*.

86-87.  For the expression *un renc cerchier*, 'to cross the lists from one end to another' in a tournament, cf. Marie de France, *Milun*, ed. J. Rychner:

> Li turneiemenz s'asemble.                397
> Ki juste quist, tost la trove;
> Ki aukes volt les rens cerchier,
> Tost i pout perdre u gaaignier
> Encuntrer un cumpainun.

90-91.  On the significance of Monday as the starting date for tournaments, see L. A. Vigneras, "Monday as a Date for

Medieval Tournaments," *MLN*, 48 (1933), 80-82, where he discusses the frequency with which knights foreswore fighting on Sundays and therefore began tournaments on Mondays. The expression, says Limentani (note to this line) is akin to wishing that every day had 48 hours, while Lecoy (in his edition) recalls a "semaine de quatre jeudis," a wistful schoolboys' expression dating from the time when French schools met Monday through Wednesday, Friday and Saturday. In 91 *il estoit* is an impersonal expression, while the following *il* refers to *lundi*.

93. *AB* read *peniu* ('long-lasting') *d'armes* to which Orr changed his edition of *E*. The expression *preu d'armes* is cited in Tobler-Lommatzsch (s.v. *pro*) with quotes from the *Roman de Troie*, 3501, *Des ses armes esteit mout proz* and *Galeran de Bretagne*, F59, *Auques preuz d'armes et hardiz*. Since there is evidence that this is not ungrammatical, I have retained the ms reading, which is also found in *DG*.

94-97. Jean Renart makes a point here of the care his hero takes in dressing appropriately. See Mary Evans, *Costume Throughout the Ages*, revised edition (Philadelphia & New York: Lippincott, 1950), pp. 33-37 where she discusses the increase in interest in fine clothing and fabrics in the eleventh and twelfth centuries as a result of travel to the East during the Crusades. An earlier manifestation of the same interest is the following description of Erec (*Erec et Enide*, ed. Roques):

> Sor un destrier estoit montez          94
> afublez d'un mantel hermin;
> galopant vient tot le chemin;
> s'ot cote d'un diapre noble
> qui fu fez an Costantinoble;
> chauces de paile avoit chauciees,
> molt bien fetes et bien tailliees.

In 96 of the *Lai, donnoit = se donnoit*; see Ménard §125c on the omission of the reflexive pronoun; cf. 721.

105. The comparison to Tristan, as model of knightly accomplishment, is one of three references to that legend in the *Lai*; cf. 124, 457. The frequency with which Jean Renart also refers to that story in his other works has led Sweetser (Introduction to his edition of the *Escoufle* (Droz, 1974), p.

xxv) to refer to that poem as an anti- or super-Tristan.

122.   *Amors*, last mentioned by name in 112, is the subject of *fist* in this line.

124.   *c'* = *qu'* with elipsis of *si* = 'si bien que, tellement que'; see Ménard § 248.  For the reference to Tristan's shaving his head (*a force* = 'with a pair of scissors') in order to impersonate a madman, see *Les deux poèmes de la Folie Tristan*, ed. J. Bédier: in the *Berne Folie, Haut fu tonduz, lonc ot lo col/A mervoille sambla bien fol* (154-155), and the Oxford, *Od* ('avec') *les forces haut se tundi/Ben senble fol u esturdi* (209-210).

135.   *que* = *car*; it is also possible that *que* = *qui* with *son cuer* as antecedent, but the confusion of *que* and *qui* is rare in this manuscript.

140-142.   On the plural subject with a singular verb, see Ménard § 128-1 who speaks of the agreement of the verb with the nearest subject.  Cf. 202-203, 215, 349, 362-363, 482-483 for other examples of this construction.

146-149.   The clause as read in *E* (147), *qu'il la connoissoit bien*, has caused some difficulty.  I have emended *E* to *qui la c-* by following the other mss and by understanding the *le* of *ABCG* as a Picard feminine weak object pronoun.  The whole passage indicates that the hero has seen the lady before and, now that Love has caused him to fall in love with her, calls upon his eyes, i.e. his memory of having seen her, as witness to his statement that he had never before seen so pleasing a person.  Cf. 344 and the note to that line.

157.   Orr emended to *A, Ceus que d'amors erent soupris*, but I feel that *E, Fet cil, qui d'amors ert seurpris* can be understood as proverbial: 'I have scorned,/He said, [him] who was surprised by love,' and have therefore retained the ms reading.

160-161.   Barbers served as surgeons through to the 18th century, and tooth pulling, as well as bleeding and other procedures, was performed by them.  See *Trésor de la langue française*, vol. 4, s.v. *barbier* where these lines of the *Lai* are cited as the oldest French reference to this double professional function, and M. Dominica Legge, "Toothache and Courtly Love," *FS*, 4 (1950), 50-54.

164. In changing the reading of *E* from *einsi* to *en si*, I am being guided by *ABF*, as was Orr. The emendation clarifies the meaning of the whole clause.

194. *E* reads *Il i avroit* where *il* is impersonal ('there would be') as opposed to *ele* in all the other mss. It is because of such distribution of variants that one might give credence to Bédier's suggestion that *E* is a version reworked by Jean Renart himself; see Introduction, p. 2 and notes to 429-439, 815.

232-233. Orr emends *sa bonté* to *la bonté* with *ABDFG* because of *De la dame* of the following line. I see *sa*, however, as an emphatic anticipation of the possessive expression which also serves to link *bonté* and the *dame* whom he loves. Cf. among other instances in *E* 550 where *le = le chevalier*, an anticipation in the singular of the objects *les soupirs, les lermes;* 573 *Qu'i li derompi son penser* where *li* anticipates the possessive adjective; and 615-616 *en son doit/Cestui. . . .*

240. For the use of *coi* as a command, cf. *Robin et Marion* 460 *Coi!* ('Be quiet!') quoted in Tobler-Lommatzsch s.v. *coi.*

242-243. For a discussion of the events alluded to in these lines, i.e. the capture of Christians by Turks during the Crusades, see L. A. Vigneras, *MPh*, 30 (1933), 351-359 and the Introduction, pp. 11-12; cf. 250-251.

244. *Aere* has been discussed by M. Roques (*Romania*, 59 (1933), 428) where he translates it as 'Hé! la! allons, allons!' —an exhortation to calm. It has been associated conjecturally by Orr in his note to this line with *a oirre* ('forthwith, now') or with the Latin etymon ITER (therefore, 'let's go!').

246. Although the needs of versification do not dictate an emendation of this regular 8-syllable line where the schwa of *me un* can be read in hiatus (see note to 27), the meaning does still demand some adverb between *un* and *mains*. All other mss have *poi*, which I have inserted here.

253-254.  *qu'en fusse seürs*, parallel to *que il fust miens*
(252) is dependent on *Par si* ('on the condition that').  It is not
entirely clear whose speech includes, 254, *Et qanqu'il a dedenz
les murs*.  Orr assigns it to the knight, while Bédier, Limentani
and Lecoy attribute it to the men, in order, explains Limentani
(note to this line), to increase the irony of their speech.  I believe
that Orr is correct, however, because 'everything inside the walls'
is a covert reference to the lady and is therefore a major part
of the knight's sophism, commented on by Jean Renart in
256-257.

263.  In emending from *ne chemin ne voie* to *n'en . . . n'en*,
I am following a suggestion made by Bédier (1913) in his note
to this line which, nevertheless, he did not emend.  More modern
editors have been divided, but *Bele dame* 264 is the direct object
of *trespasser* ('ignore, pass by without acknowledging').  As
confirming evidence, cf. Tobler-Lommatzsch s.v. *trespasser*
where are cited as objects of this verb geographic or physical
entities which can be traversed, such as woods, mountains,
countries, valleys, but not roads.

267.  The use of the indicative *alons* after *veil et lo* (266)
emphasizes the strong likelihood in the mind of the knight
that his party will indeed go to the castle.

268-269.  The subject of *guenchissent*, 3rd person plural,
is *chascuns*, a singular.  The reading, which occurs in all the mss,
reflects the fact that while they all act together, each man turns
the head of his own horse.

270-271.  Mss *ABE* read *as armes*, and *CGDF* have *aus
dames*, a parody of the battle cry which also occurs in *Guillaume
de Dole* 223.  Orr emended *E* to *dames*, but I feel *as armes* can
be retained to underline Jean Renart's use of *tencon* ('contrast,
quarrel') in 271.  The real battle cry prefigures the debate, which
verges on a contest or even quarrel in the lines to come.  See
Ph. Ménard, *Le rire et le sourire dans le roman courtois en
France au moyen âge (1150-1250)* (Droz, 1969), p. 518 for a
discussion of this passage.

277-279.  For further discussion of clothing in the Middle
Ages for both men and women, see E. R. Goddard, *Women's*

*Costume in French Texts of the Eleventh and Twelfth Centuries* (The Johns Hopkins Press, 1927); s. v. *chaisne*, p. 314.

288-289.   The valets who hold the stirrups (*estriers*) are those who rode with the hero and his companions, cf. 215: *Il monte et vallet jusqu'a sis.*   Each knight has a valet on each side to help him dismount.   *A* reads *estres*, interpreted by Bédier (1913) as 'balcon, galérie,' which would make the valets members of the lady's household.   Limentani keeps that reading and interpretation, but Lecoy corrects to *estriers*, noting "une faute banale (oubli d'un signe d'abréviation)."

292.   *E* is alone in reading *s'en tort*, which I have emended to *s'en cort* in accordance with all the other mss.   *cort* is the present indicative of *corir*, which fits better than *tort*, a subjunctive form of *torner* in a context where there is no reason for a subjunctive.   I have also emended *ere* to *ert* for the needs of the meter, despite other third person singular forms in the *Lai* with final -*e*: *iere* 53, *ere* 882.

299-300.   For a discussion of *trecie: drecie*, Picard feminine past participles of verbs in -*ier*, see the language description, p. 17; cf. 593-594.

305.   *ci* = *si*.

306.   For *que que* and the indicative, see Ménard §78, rem. 3 where he has indicated that *que que* followed by the subjunctive has concessive meaning ('although') as contrasted to the indicative with temporal force ('while').   The passage here seems rather ambiguous to the modern reader, but all the mss have the indicative, therefore temporal, meaning.

308.   With Orr I have emended from *venir* to *issir* with *ABDF*, to avoid an identical rhyme and to improve the meaning slightly, although *venir* certainly makes admissible sense.

311.   *Li* = 'à la dame'; *il* is an impersonal: the arrival of the knights is pleasing to the lady.   With Orr I have emended *sa* to *lor*, the reading of all the other mss, since the 3rd person reference *lor* is to all three of the men, as should be the mention of their arrival in the same clause.

314.  *chainse*: cf. note to 277-279 on items of clothing in the Middle Ages.

317.  On the use of reeds as floor covering, Tobler-Lommatzsch s.v. *jonc* cite the *Comte de Poitiers* 315: *Les greg-nors tors et les plus beles/Coisirent avec les puceles/De vers cendaus furent celees/De joins furent desous pavees*, and *Hunbaut* 3076: *De vers jons ont fait lor seir/Covers de bon vers dras de soie*.

320.  *qui = cui; ait* is impersonal.

344-348.  Like lines 146-149 (cf. note) these lines make good sense if one supposes that the knight has seen the lady before, from a distance: his heart, which was firmly settled in her, took them (= his eyes, 343) as witness (i.e. recognized their truthfulness), for whatever they had promised him, they now were testifying convincingly (well) that they had lied to him about nothing.  There is a clear reference here to lines 146-149, since the lady's beauty seen close-up confirms his previous glimpse of her.

366-367.  'For those who strive for nothing except to be a loyal lover.'

370.  Following Orr's interpretation, I have understood *sifet* as one word meaning 'such.'  The line means, therefore, 'It is very astonishing! Whence (comes) such a statement?'  The style, in broken expressions of surprise, mirrors the reaction of the lady to the knight's declaration, totally unexpected by her.  See note to 700-705.

382-387.  This complicated passage is best understood by interpreting 382-383 as an apposition to *vos* of 384; the lady is speaking directly to the knight and, by describing his physical beauty as well as stating that he could fool her (*trere la plume par mi l'ueil*) with words, she is announcing that she is on her guard against the danger of being persuaded to do what she should not.

429-433.  The reading of *E* differs radically from that of the other mss; see variant readings.  In *E*,

> Quant aucune dame vaillant
> Fet aucun chevalier semblant
> De cortoisie et d'ennor fere
> Lors cuident tot lor autre afere . . .

the lady places blame on men for misinterpreting the courtesy and respect of the lady. In *A,* on the other hand, the lady blames women for unfairly encouraging suitors by not noticing or understanding their intentions:

> Por c'est fole chose de nous,
> dames, qui sons mal parcevanz:
> quant cortoisie et biaus sanblanz
> nous maine a cortoisie fere,
> lors cuident . . .

Like 194 (cf. note), this passage may be evidence that Jean Renart reworked the text of *E* himself; see note to 815.

447. *ait* is in the subjunctive mood by attraction, indirectly dependent on *ainz que* (446-447) which governs *se vant.*

451. *que = ce que*; cf. 111 and see Ménard §65.

456-457. For the story of Tristan's setting out to sea in a boat without a mast, see J. Bédier, *Le Roman de Tristan et Iseut* (Paris, [1926], p. 22). The section was taken from the *Tristan* of Eilhart von Oberg. See note to 105 for a discussion of Jean Renart's frequent use of this legend. On *aussi con* 'ainsi que' see Godefroy, I, 238 s.v. *alsi* where the confusion of the two conjunctions is noted.

463. *nule* = 'nulle nuit'; the knight is threatening to die (i.e. not to see another nightfall) if he does not receive the love of the lady this very night. The rhyme *anuit: anuit* is a clever one: it seems identical at first and then the audience becomes aware of the fact that Jean Renart has rhymed an adverb and a third person present subjunctive form.

475. For a discussion of the presence of written schwa /ə/ and elision, see note to 27.

486-487. Previous editors have disagreed over the reference of *ses cuers*, 'his' or 'her heart.' With Lecoy and Limentani, and contrary to the position of Orr, I believe that the knight is referred to: his heart is not lying to her (*li* 485), i.e. he is being sincere. For further discussion, see Lecoy's note to this line.

492-501. The lady is contradicting here the first "rule" of love in Andreas Capellanus's *De Amore* (Munich: Eidos, 1964) which states (p. 310) "Causa coniugii ab amore non est excusatio recta," a spouse is no excuse for not loving. The knight hastens to point this fact out to her (500ff); she will gain honor through love, accompanied though it might be by infidelity to her husband. My emendation in 498 from *Il* to *Mes* is suggested by the meaning of the passage since an adversative is appropriate to the knight's argument that although her husband must be made very happy by her loyalty, he, on the other hand, does not believe she would be badly judged by others. See the *De Amore*, pp. 271-295, "De variis iudiciis amoris," on various judgments about love, for a report of questions and answers on the ethics of love. On the same question, see B. N. Sargent, "The *Lai de l'ombre* and the *De Amore*," *RomN*, 7 (1965-1966), 73-79.

504-505. On the importance of pilgrimages and a mendicant existence as forms of penance, see J.-C. Payen, *Le Motif du Repentir dans la littérature française médievale* (Genève: Droz, 1967), pp. 44-49.

510. *s'* = *c'*; cf. 305, 529.

513. I have followed Orr in emending from *fetes* to *dites* to conform to all the other mss. *Fere* for *dire* is used most often to report speech directly, and the scribe may have written *fetes* both because of *fet* in the preceding line and *fetes* in the following, both roughly in the middle of the line.

512-517. Orr changes the order of the two verbs in this passage so that instead of *Recevez moi par un joel . . . Ou vos retenez un des miens*, *Retenez* now has *moi* as its object, defining the position the knight hopes to achieve vis-à-vis the lady, while *recevez* has the ring or belt as an object. While the emendation is not strictly necessary, it makes for smoother reading. Since one can also see how a scribe could confuse these two imperative forms which begin and end with the same syllables and have the same structure, I have followed Orr in making the emendation.

521.  For the emendation from *n'en* to *ne* I have followed Orr.  The verb *face* takes a direct object (understood here) parallel to 518-519: *biens/Que chevalier face.*

526-527.  The lady's statement that she does not want praise without profit is not immediately clear.  The *lox* ('praise, honor, glory') would come from the service the knight has promised her above (518-521).  For *preu*, see Schultz-Gora (*Archiv*, 164 (1933), p. 45) who suggests that any profit would be for the knight, but, since the lady is not interested in giving her love (530-533), he would be cheated of the advantage to be gained by serving her.  Lecoy (note to this passage) explains the eliptical nature of the statement as a delicate way of talking about gain for either of them.

547.  *le = la*. See language description, p. 19 for a discussion of Picard traits in this text.  Cf. 558, and 147 with its note.

550-551.  For a discussion of *le* as an emphatic anticipation of the multiple direct objects, see note to 232.

552-553.  *li* refers to the knight in both lines.  The lady, who is thinking to herself, is analyzing the emotions of her suitor.

564.  The subject of *a . . . mostree* is *Amors* (566); love shows him the way to do a courteous act by the very fact of the lady's being lost in a revery.  Note the opposition of *Amors* and *Resons* (559).  The personification of Love and Reason traditionally show internal debate either because two people are disagreeing with each other or because of conflict in one person's mind.  A notable example among many is the *Chevalier de la Charrete*, ed. Roques, 365-377, where Lancelot is resolving his internal conflict about getting into the cart with the dwarf.

573-574.  See note to 232 for a discussion of the syntax of *li* as anticipation (573).  On the indicative *lut* after *que* (= *tant que*), see Ménard § 247-1, 156d who says that result clauses take the indicative if the result has been attained.  Cf. 639 for a similar construction and 692 for the counter-situation, a non-attained result clause with the subjunctive.  See notes to 74-77, 306, for *que* in place of a full compound conjunction.

593-594.   For a discussion of the Picard feminine past participles at the rhyme, see the language description, p. 17. Cf. 299-300, and note.

597.   *E* reads *meinscroire* which I have emended to *mescroire* to follow *ABCFG*. It is hard to find a meaning for *meinscroire* as a single word, which Orr and Levy gloss as 'ne pas croire' as if it were *mescroire*. I believe it is rather a scribal error.

606.   I have emended the ms reading *manmel* to *manel* 'little finger.'   For a discussion of this word, see M. D. Legge, "Le doit mainuel" in *Studi in onore di Angelo Monteverde* (Modena, 1959), pp. 390-391, where she argues convincingly that Jean Renart, by using an enjambement with *De son pié* of the next line, is expressing wittily the fact that the lady turns pale from head to toe.   Given the difficulty of interpreting this line, it is not surprising that the variant readings differ widely: *B menouel, C menuel, D cervel, F mamel, G meniel*. It is not clear what *BCG* mean, while *D* and *F* are clearly attempts to make sense of this line without accounting for *De son pié* of 607.

615-616.   For a discussion of the syntax of *son . . . Cestui* see note to 232.

621-622.   *l' = li = le li.*   See Ménard §50-1 and Foulet, *Petite Syntaxe* §203 on the frequent use of the third person indirect object in what would otherwise be a double object construction.   Cf. 834.   In 622 *me = le me* and in 937 *vos = le vos*, rarer omissions with a first or second person indirect object, to be compared with 733 *le me donnastes*, a full double-object construction.   *Art* (621) refers to the art of flirtation and even trickery.

623.   *soutise* is a hapax.   It could be the feminine of *soutil* or *soutif*, which would make it an adjustment for the rhyme with *prise* from *soutile* or *soutive*.   It may also be a feminine form based on a masculine *soutis*, also unattested.   Again (as in 606, see note), the variants attest to some confusion among

the scribes: *AB si prise, CDFG si sorprise*.

634-635.  The thought expressed in these lines by the words of the lady are reflected in the similar language of 670-671, spoken by the knight.

650. *cui = que*.

660-661.  Orr reads these lines to mean that the knight is interpreting his being sent after as the lady's eagerness to see him again.  *Ce* (660) is therefore an anticipation of the whole of 661, *Qu'il tarde cele qu'el le voie*.  For other examples, cf. 665-666, 780-781.  The second half of 661 is elliptical, with omission of *tant, jusqu'a ce* or another temporal conjunction (cf. note to 74-77) which would govern the subjunctive.

669.  *Citiaus* is a reference to the Trappist order at Cîteaux, where very strict observance of monastic rule was kept.  The knight is saying, therefore, that he would give up his entire worldly existence rather than take back the ring.

700-705.  The syntax of this passage is not entirely coherent.  Lecoy explains it as a reflection of the lady's perturbed state.  Orr, later quoted by Limentani, sees it as coherent, but ironic, and admits he is unable to explain the *ainçois* (704) which repeats *ja* (702).  There are no significant variants in the other mss, and Lecoy's reading of incoherence parallel to a mental state is the most convincing argument to date.  Cf. note to 370 where incoherence and surprise are also expressed syntactically.  Bédier (1929) sees an ellipsis after *parlement* (703), but since all of the mss generally agree, the omission of one or more lines is highly conjectural.

712-713.  We never learn what happens to the knight's and lady's attendants in the ensuing intimate scene.  Do they not bother him because they have discretely withdrawn, or because he is unconscious of them?  This problem is one of the very few unresolved questions in this unusually tightly constructed tale (another might be the lady's husband).

716-717.  The expression *l'a . . . ferue du poing lez l'oie* comes as a surprisingly abrupt change of tone in what is generally a courtly passage. It is equivalent to 'you could have hit me (her) with a ton of bricks' and has been cited, in notes by Orr and Limentani, as an example of Jean Renart's down-to-earth turns of phrase.

721.  The reflexive pronoun *nos* is understood; cf. 96 and note.

726-727.  Orr and Levy take *preu* to be an adverb which they translate respectively as 'well' and 'suffisamment.' Frappier, in his review of Orr (*RLR*, 71 (1951), 78-79), sees it as a noun and translates 'il n'y a pas encore dans sa poursuite (*en la trace* évoque l'idée de la chasse, comme la var. *en la nasse* celle de la pêche) de profit, d'avantage dont il doive se réjouir.' The variant readings reflect the lack of clarity surrounding the last word of this line: *ABDG nasse, C bien aisse, F a ce.* I have emended *Il* (726) to *mes*-adversative following Lecoy's note and mss *CGDF.*

733.  On the double pronoun order, see note to 621-622; cf. 798.

743.  The past participial form *reçut* shows final *-t* which Moignet (*Grammaire de l'ancien français.* [Paris, 1973], p. 58) marks as archaic and/or regionally situated in the north and northeast of France. He further suggests that it shows spelling tradition.

754.  On (*ja*) *mar* and the future with negative value, cf. *Chanson de Roland* 196 *Ja mar creirez Marsilie; Livre des rois* 41 *Mar avrez pour*, etc. quoted by Tobler-Lommatzsch s.v. *mar*; cf. 780.

759.  I have emended *ert* to *est* despite *F c'estoit* since *F* is a frequently inaccurate and unclear text, and the knight is talking about his situation at the moment. One can easily see the scribal error happening as an anticipation of the medial letters of *certes* later in the line.

778-781.  With Orr I have emended *baerez* (780) to *baeroit* following *D* and thus providing *Nule du mont* (781) a function as subject of the verb. On *baer a*, see Tobler-Lommatzsch s.v.

*baer: baer a folie, Auc.* 10, 42, . . . *ne be pas a entamer/Mon testament por autre amer, Roman de la Rose* 7662. The four lines in the *Lai* mean, therefore, 'The force of love for you engulfs me and places me in great distress, nor would any women in the world urge this, that I take it back.' Cf. 660-661 and its note on the anticipatory *ce*.

815. The expression *chanter de Renart* has caused much discussion. It stands alone among the mss as opposed to *de Bernart*, an expression attested in the form *parler d'autre Bernart*, and its more frequent *parler d'autre Martin* meaning 'to change tone.' Lecoy's note on the expression (in his glossary, s.v. *chanter*) points out other instances where *Renart* is a variant of *Bernart*. Jean Renart is certainly not averse to puns (see notes to 46-49 and 962) and barely veiled allusions to himself and his work (cf. 21-24 and note). Is this another small bit of evidence suggesting that Jean Renart rewrote *E* himself? See notes to 194, 429-439.

822-823. I have followed Orr in emending 822 *Que por parole que je die* to the reading of the other mss *Quant parole que je vos die*, thereby providing a subject for *puet* (823), which otherwise would not have one. It is possible that the scribe of *E* copied what was a first person verb as a third person form (*puet*), thereby causing the confused syntax.

832-833. *geu parti* is being used here in the sense of 'choice,' not necessarily 'game' or 'competition' as it often is in Old French. It is linked etymologically to *partir* ('separate, choose sides'). It later evolved to designate what occurs after one has chosen a side, therefore a game; see A. Långfors et al., eds. *Recueil général des jeux-partis français* (SATF, 1926) and especially pp. v-x of the Introduction.

835. On the omission of the conjunction *que*, see Ménard §199a who indicates the frequency of this construction, especially in twelfth-century epic poems, but also elsewhere (as here) for the needs of the meter.

836-837. This proverb (Morawski 2294) expresses the idea of pushing things too far: if the knight insists too much he will totally destroy what he wants to gain.

858. This line has raised some questions, first about the reference of *na* (*AB nel*). Tobler, in a review of Bédier (1890) (*Archiv*, 85 (1890), 357), suggested that the knight did not name the ring, i.e. did not use the possessive 'my' or 'your' in designating it. It is also possible, and perhaps more probable, that *AB nel* is a Picard form, meaning *ne la* (see note to 593-594) and referring to the lady. For *na* (= *ne + la*), see the *Glossary of the First Continuation* (by L. Foulet, vol. III, pt. 2 of the *Perceval Continuations*), s.v. *na*, with its notes and references. Bédier (1929) divides the words differently as *n'anoma pas* 'he did not name (her).' One then has to understand a direct object pronoun. For *anomer*, for *nomer* 'to name,' see Godefroy, I, 298a, s.v. *anomer: Par cel segnor, qi Dex est anomez,/Ge nel feroie por quanqe vos avez, Roncisv.*, p. 17, ed. Bourdillon. But the whole line makes very little sense. As Lecoy points out, no names have been used throughout; why suddenly and pointlessly announce that the knight does not use her name? I am forced to agree with Orr (note to this line) that the line is "rather a weak piece of padding."

868. *enprenant* = *esprenant*; cf. 887. Substitution of prefixes is frequent but sporadic in Old French; cf. 183, 912 for forms of *esprendre*.

876. On the tautological *plus greingnor*, cf. *on li faisoit . . . honnor/Asses plus c'as autres grinour, Ch. II esp.*, 196 and *Par sex mois, par ung an ou par temps plus grigneur, Gir Ross,* 47, both quoted in Tobler-Lommatzsch, s.v. *graignor.*

883. The imperfect *amot* is an eastern form used at the rhyme with *mot.* See Nyrop, *Grammaire historique de la langue française* (5$^e$ ed., Copenhagen, 1924), vol. II, 157$_2$, and cf. 147: 148 *amoit:voit* for another imperfect form at the rhyme.

884. The phrase *tot a un mot* means, according to Tobler-Lommatzsch s.v. *mot* 'in one word,' therefore 'immediately.' They quote *Escan* 14405: *Li rois Artus . . . fist ses compaignons savoir/Qu'il moveroit le bien matin . . . /Et si vouz di que volen-tiers/I alerent tuit a un mot . . .* It is unclear whether the knight says the phrase (as R. Levy [rev. of Bédier 1913, 1929 in *Romania*, 58 (1932), 436-441], Orr, Levy and Limentani) or if it is adverbial, modifying *fet* and describing the speed with

which the knight answered (as Bédier). I am inclined to make it part of his speech, but the arguments are not overwhelming in either direction.

887. *empres* = *apres*; see note to 868 on prefix substitution.

892. All other editors have placed *en non Deu* with the speech of the knight. I prefer it as part of the lady's speech, to add some exasperation to her reaction: he has just told her he has a successor picked out to receive the ring and she is not only curious, but a bit hurt at the speed with which he has done so.

904-907. *Car* introduces a regret or wish (see Moignet, *Grammaire de l'ancien français*, p. 289, Ménard §153, rem. 4), here a negative idea: "[It is a] pity that there isn't a gate. . . ." On *dire*, meaning 'one can say,' see Tobler, *Vermischte Beiträge*, 3rd ed., I, pp. 91-95. The whole passage, therefore, means "Pity there is no gate or door down there! Thus she could come up here so that one could express his thanks for the honor she has done me."

932. Bédier changed *vostre cuer . . . el mien* to *mon cuer . . . el vostre* which would mean that her love has been gained. But the change is not necessary. Putting the knight's heart into hers can be an indication that she now accepts it there.

937. *vos* = *le vos* with omission of the direct object pronoun; see note to 621-622.

938. Orr and Bédier both emended this line from *Je cuit que vos ne l'avrez mie* to the reading of *ABF: Je cuit vos ne l'amerez mie* which is more immediately understandable. In Tobler-Lommatzsch, however, s.v. (*bien*) *avoir* is the transitive meaning 'to like something.' I believe the line here has that meaning, even without *bien*: "I believe you will not like it/Less than yours . . ." and have therefore not emended the line. Cf. *Escanor*, as quoted in Tobler-Lommatzsch, 19940: *Mais li biauz Escanors avoir/Les savoit mout bien et l'amoient. . . .*

947. Orr emends *parole* to *partie*, noting a scribal mis-

understanding. In doing so he follows *CG*, while *ABDF* have *lor part*. But *parole* can be understood to mean 'communication,' rather than the articulated 'word,' and I have therefore not emended the line.

952. With Orr I have emended *a rien* to *de rien* following mss. *ABCDG*. The scribe took *rien* as the object of *penser* despite *a lor afere* of the following line, and thus misunderstood *de rien*, adverb, meaning 'ever, at any time.'

958. A hole at the left of the column makes the first letter of this line illegible. It was probably 7 = *Et*, but any addition would make the line hypersyllabic. Since the meaning has not been obscured by the omission, no emendation based on a conjecture as to the nature of the missing initial letter is necessary.

962. In addition to the pun here, cf. 20:21 *bon*, 45:46 *rimer* (and note), 255 *sire*, 389:90 *conte*, 815 *Renart* (and note). Other rhymes, like 953:954 *afere: a fere*, while not puns, also show Jean Renart's evident pleasure in playing with language; see Introduction, p. 15.

# INDEX OF PROPER NAMES

All references to personal and place names have been given, as well as all instances of personification. An asterisk after a line number refers to a note in the commentary. Since the protagonists are nameless, and since there are so few characters in the *Lai*, I have not included references to them as *dame, chevalier* or *sire*.

# GLOSSARY

Included are all words which are not found in standard Modern French, either because of meaning or form. All instances are cited. Verbs are cited in the infinitive, which is enclosed in brackets when that form is not attested in the text. Necessary conjugated forms are numbered 1-6, instead of 1-3 singular and plural. An asterisk after a line number refers to the commentary.

a *prep: loc* a ce que 576 while; 623 whereas, because
aage *m* 117 existence, life
aatir *tr* 505 to compare
achoison *m* 659 reason, cause
acointance *f* 791 friendship, acquaintance
acointe *adj* 67 familiar, intimate
[acointier] *refl* 663 to get to know
[acoler] *tr* 178 to hug
aconjurer *tr* 824, 844 to implore, beseech
[acouter] *refl* 878 to lean against
[acuser] *refl* 32 to disclose one's identity, become evident
adés *adv* 342 at once
adonques *adv* 790 then, next
aere *interj* 244*
afere *m* 88, 337, 434, 460, 566, 645, 854, 910, 953 situation, interest; 335 things (indef)
ahan *m* 126 pain, torment
ahi *interj* 152, 594 alas
aïe 612 *imper 2*; aït 521, 747, 805 *pres subj 3 of* aidier *tr* to help
ainçois, ançois *adv* 2, 704*, 745, 840 rather; *prep* 236, 416 before; *conj* 308, 668 before
ainz *adv* 297, 337, 398, 486, 502, 552, 630, 688, 751, 784, 886 rather; *with neg* 574 never; a- mes 467 *v* mes; *conj* 190, 446*, 728, 816 before
alaschier *tr* 171 to relieve, ease
alers *m* 199 act of going, trip
ambedui *num adj* 319, 581 both

amender *tr* 902 to improve; *loc* son oirre a- 660 to hasten his step

[amesurer] *tr* 34 to temper, restrain

ançois *v* ainçois

andui *adj* 942, 959; andeus 957 both

anel, aneaus *m* 516, 571, 575, 605, 613, 625, 658, 667, 724, 732, 751, 767, 788, 864, 894, 899, 923, 928 ring

anelet *m* 682 little ring

angoisseus *adj* 161 in pain, distress

anoree *v* ennorer

anui *m* 690, 713, 763, 797 trouble, bother

anuit 462\* *pres subj 3 of* anuyer, enuyer *tr* to trouble, disturb

anuit *adv* 461\* tonight

[aovrer] *refl* 9\* to put oneself to work

[aparler] *tr* 340 to address

apenser *tr* 574; *refl* 220 to wonder, bring to mind

[aporter] *tr* 267 to recommend

apris *adj* 330 brought up

aqueut 723 *pres ind 3 of* accueillir *tr* to welcome

art 23, 183 *pres ind 3 of* ardoir *tr;* 23 to burn, consume; 183 to make s.o. passionate

as = a + les *art* 82, 100, 107, 229, 243, 270, 289, 364, 418, 481

[asener] *tr* 908 to succeed, achieve (a goal)

asis *adj* 252 assigned, deeded

[assentir] *refl* 402 to agree

assez *adv* 430, 591 very, greatly

atant *adv* 268, 604, 636, 648, 706, 960 then, at that moment

[ataster] *tr* 182 to touch, feel for

atorner *tr* 854 to arrange; *refl* 212 to prepare oneself

[atraire] *tr* 204 to say, pronounce

aucun *adj* 7, 10, 14, 431, 432, 543 some, any; *indef pron* 51 someone

auques *indef pron* 328 something

aussi *adv: loc* a- con 457\* just like

autretel *adv* 280 equally, in the same way

aval *adv* 679 downward, down

[avaler] *intr* 288 to climb down, dismount

[avenir] *intr* 185, 430, 807, 919 to happen

aveques *prep* 333 with

averté *f* 152 avarice, unwillingness to give

avis *m: loc* estre a- 142, 484 to seem

[aviver] *intr* 374 to animate, give life

[avoir] *impers* 11, 73, 172, 194, 200, 239, 254, 320, 453, 795, 888, 904 there is, are; *tr* 938 to value, esteem; *refl* 71 to behave; *loc* ce i

a- 744, 745, 819 to be a question of

[baer] *intr* 780* to pay attention to, notice
baille *m* 274 hold, outer court (of a castle)
bailleu *m* 121 bailiff, administrative servant
barbier *m* 160* barber
bastir *v* plet
bel *adj* 278, 863 handsome, beautiful; *adv* 603, 723, 787, 927 well; *loc*
    estre b- a 311 to be pleasing, welcome
belement *adv* 245 nicely, gently
[blecier] *tr* 930 to insult, hurt (the feelings of)
bon *adj: loc* estre des b- 21 to be of high birth
buer *adv* 654, 908 at a good time, well


c' *v* que
car *conj* 176, 413, 904* *introduces a wish*
[celer] *tr* 223 to hide
cherchier *tr: loc* un renc c- 86-87* to seek an opponent (at a tournament)
    by going up and down a line of contenders
certes *adv* 156, 377, 472, 488 surely; *loc* a c- 77, 588, 759 seriously
chainse *m* 314* linen feminine garment, tunic
chantel *m: loc* en c- 277 to one side
chanter de Renard 815*
chapel *m* 282 crown
cheoir *m* 899 fall; choïr *intr* 547 to fall
chief *m* 85, 811 head; *loc* de c- en c- 86 from one end to another; venir a
    c- 812, 959 to finish, come to an end
chier *adj* 172 dear; *loc* avoir c- 642, 827 to cherish
chiere *f* 349 appearance
choïr *v* cheoir
chois *m: loc* a son c- 58 at one's command
[choisir] *tr* 605 to perceive, notice
ci *adv* 52, 53, 360, 611, 732, 888, 905 here
cil *demon adj/pron* 59, 94, 157, 265, 294, 342, 390, 448, 570, 580, 706,
    757, 852 he; 234, 262, 307 they
cler *adj* 141, 522 beautiful; 881 clear, shining
clos *p p of* clore *tr* closed in
coi *adj* 240* peaceful, still
cointe *adj* 68 reserved, inaccessible
col *m* 177, 303, 817 neck
colon *m* 439 dove
comment *conj* 458 although

con *conj* 24, 227, 241, 305, 379, 390, 411, 441, 457, 711 as, like; 230, 312, 445, 694, 827 that

[confondre] *tr* 776 to destroy, undo

congié *m* 465 permission, leave; *loc* a vo c- 577 with your permission

conroi *m: loc* prendre c- 542 to take care of, see to

consant 600 *pres subj 3 of* conseillier *tr* to help

conte 389 *v* desfere

[conter] *tr* 305 to tell, recount; 962* to calculate, reckon

contreval *adv* 483 downward

[corir] *intr: loc* c- seure 113, 552, 778 to attack, invade

cors *m* 108, 129, 183, 382, 419 body

cort *f* 291, 681, 709 courtyard

coute *f* 298 cushion, pillow

coutel *m* 773 knife

couvent, covent *m* 860 promise, agreement; 485 *v* fausser; *loc* par c- 865 on condition

[covenir] *intr* 137, 542, 794, 829, 952 to be suitable, to be necessary; 951 to be placed in the keeping, under the care of

creance *f* 807 belief, opinion

[creanter] *tr* 518 to swear, promise

cri *m* 748 rumor

cuer *m* 131, 135, 196, 207, 345, 351, 464, 481, 486*, 508, 533, 719, 785, 788, 868, 932*, 945, 957 heart

cui *rel pron dat* 160, 650 to, for whom

[cuidier] *tr* 18, 56, 198, 434, 462, 471, 490, 590, 619, 634, 646, 670, 724, 757, 840, 874, 938 to believe, think; cuidier *m* 422 belief, certainty

cuivre *m or f* 331 disturbance

dangier *m* 396, 524 domination, power; 153, 684 refusal

debonere, debonnere *adj* 19, 79, 338, 444, 554 good natured, kind, gracious

debonneretez *f* 140, 452 friendliness, kindness

deceüe *pp as adj* 530, deceitful

dedenz *prep* 254 inside

deduire *tr* 681 to amuse; *refl* 334, 721 to enjoy oneself

deduit *m* 116, 170 pleasure, enjoyment; 102 sport

degré *m* 679 step (of a flight of stairs)

deïsse 214 *perf subj 1 of* dire (*q.v.*)

delez *prep* 329 next to

delié *adj* 314 delicate, fine

delit *m* 42 pleasure, enjoyment

[delitier] *tr* 44, 181 to please

demainne *m* 65 what is proper to someone

[demener] *tr* 66 to display, practice

demorer *intr* 468 to remain, go no further; *tr* 926 to keep waiting

[departir] *refl* 583 to leave, depart

[derompre] *tr* 573 to interrupt

[desaamer] *tr* 156 to look down on, disdain

desaüser *refl* 1 to lose the habit, dishabituate

descouvrir *tr* 401 to uncover, reveal

desdire *tr* 397 to deny

[desembracier] *tr* 180 to take from the embrace

[deservir] *tr* 247, 705 to merit, deserve

deseure, desor *prep* 298, 688 on, above; *loc* estre au d- 114, 777 to have
    the upper hand

desfendant: *loc* sor son cor d- 677 despite herself

[desfere] *tr* 389 to undo, upset; *refl* 900 to dissolve

[deshetier] *refl* 756 to grieve

[despecier] *tr* 22 to dismember, tear into pieces

[despendre] *tr* 33 to spend, use up

[desperer] *refl* 756 to despair

desploier *tr* 39 to spend, employ

[despriser] *tr* 103 to disdain, despise

[destraindre] *intr* 491, 650 to destroy, cause anguish

destrece *f* 191, 676, 779 pain, torment

destruire *tr* 5 to destroy

[desvoiier] *tr* 218 to lead astray

deüst 419, 875 *perf subj 3 of* devoir

devant *adv* 918; *conj* 208 before (*temporal*)

devise *f: loc* a la d- 786 according to wishes, desire of someone

dire *intr* 2, 89 to speak; distrent 322 *pret 6; m* 256 speech, words

dit *m* 7, 370, 448 speech, words

ditié *m* 466 gesture with the finger?

doing 937 *pres ind 1 of* doner *tr* to give

doit   *m*   16, 570, 575, 606, 615, 658, 682, 739, 863, 873; doi 625, 846,
    936 finger

donques *adv* 261, 762, 864; dont 694, 698 then

dont *interrog adv* 370 from where?

doz *adj* 79, 130, 933 charming, noble

[drecier] *refl* 300* to stand up

droiz *adj: loc* estre d- 196, 492 to be suitable, correct

dues *m* 806 grief, pain

dui *adj* 712 two

durement *adv* 75, 429, 704 strongly, much; 246 harshly

dusque *prep* 129, 606, 647 up to, as far as

e 6 *pres ind 1 of* avoir

el *indef pron* 3, 163, 536, 745 other, anything else

el *pron f* 167, 550, 661, 667, 723, 830 she

el = en + le *art* 131, 238, 342, 571, 575, 875, 932

em = en *prep* 37, 49, 648

emparlé *adj* 68 talkative

[emprendre] *tr* 38 to undertake; 76 *v* esprendre

emprist *v* esprendre

en = on *pron* 101, 102, 305

en *prep* 181 with respect to

[encombrer] *tr* 51 to hinder

encontre *adv* 288, 306 in that direction; *prep* 313 towards

encor *conj* 862, 939 although, even if

endroit *adv: loc* or e- 616, 630 just now; d'e- ce que 548 with respect to

ennor *m* 433; enor 849 honor, hommage

[ennorer] *tr* 474, 495, 843 to honor, respect

enpalie *adj* 611 palid, pale

enprenant *v* esprendre

enprés *prep* 887* after

enresdie *f* 821 stubbornness, recalcitrance

entendre *tr* 256, 391, 424, 437 to understand; *intr* 366, 387 to be intent on, seek to do

entor *prep* 81 near, in the vicinity of; 177 around

[entrelaïier] *tr* 35 to renounce

entremetre *refl* 475 to be occupied, busy

[entrepaistre] *refl* 944 to feed each other

entrueus *conj* 119; entrus 568 while

envielliz *adj* 866 aged

[envoisier] *refl* 942 to enjoy oneself, be merry

enz *adv* 923 inside

erranment *adv* 570, 580 promptly, quickly

es = en + les *art* 913

[esbahir] *refl* 608 to be astonished

eschés *m* 104 chess

escolfle *m* 23* kite, kind of hawk

escremie *f* 104 fencing

escureus *m* 279 squirrel (fur as trimming)

esfacier *tr* 866 to deface, damage

[esforcier] *tr* 797 to press hard, force

[esgarder] *tr* 708 to observe, follow (with one's eyes)

esgaree *adj* 473 lost and abandoned

esjoïr *refl* 727 to rejoice

[eslire] *tr* 41, 43, 65 to choose

esmovoir *tr* 211 to urge, incite

esperon *m* 283 spur; *loc* a e- 272, 648 spurred on, quickly

esploitier *tr* 442 to accomplish, bring about

esprendre *tr* 183, 868*, 912 to excite; *refl* 793 to become excited; 76 to become attracted

[esprouver] *tr* 436 to prove, demonstrate

estant: *loc* en e- 300 standing

estout *adj* 84 daring, bold

[estraindre] *tr* 179 to embrace, squeeze; 836, 837 to compress, squeeze

estre *m* 706 courtyard

estrier *m* 289* stirrup

[estriver] *intr* 48 to fight, dispute

estruire *tr* 6 to build, erect

estuet 132, 187, 536 *pres ind 3 of* estovoir *impers* to be necessary

[esvanoïr] *intr* 607 to drain away, empty

esveilliers *m* 180 awakening

eulz *m* 143, 343, 403, 481; euls 913; euz 197; oel 946 eyes

eür *m* 230 destiny, fate; 27, 37 good luck

eure *f* 408 hour; *loc* de bone e- 20 with good luck, a bone e- 496 good luck!

[faillir] *intr* 454 to lose

faintié *f* 400, 550, 737 pretense, dissimulation

faintise *f* 411 pretense

[fausser] *intr: loc* f- de couvent 485 to break a promise, an agreement

fel 14*; felon 19 *m* unrefined person, person of low birth

fere *intr* 627, 711, 865 *verbum vicarius*; 152, 157, 166, 226, 234, 240, 255, 257, 262, 265, 351, 369, 371, 423, 451, 467, 496, 507, 512, 527, 537, 577, 586, 612, 646, 671, 685, 714, 720, 730, 734, 745, 758, 762, 772, 789, 815, 820, 832, 873, 884, 888, 895, 901, 940 to say; *refl* 313 to become; *loc* si f- 795, 801 *contradictory affirmation*; non f- 795 *strong negation*

[ferir] *tr* 717*; *refl* 772 to strike

ferré *adj* 332 hammered (*for a metal*)

ferté *f* 273 fortress

fesist 164, 489, 941 *imperf subj 3*; feïsse *imperf subj 1 of* fere

fil *m* 60 son

fin 190 *pres subj 1 of* finir

fine  289  *v* reson

fol  *adj*  12, 48, 125 mad, foolish; *loc* a f- 30 foolishly, without thought

force  *f*  124* pair of scissors

force  *f*  123, 351, 355, 525, 552, 778 power, passion; *loc* a f- 803; par f-
798 by brute strength

fors  *prep*  556, 582 except, besides; f- de 950 outside of, besides; *adv.* 720
outside; ne . . . f- 172, 259, 768 only; f- que 145 (*after neg*) except

[forvoiier]  *intr*  751 to go astray

fox  *v* fol

frain  *m*: *loc*  sou f- 272 with the horse well in hand, held by the reins

franchise  *f*  499 nobility of character

frans  *adj*  79, 109 noble

fuer  *v* fors


[gaber]  *intr*  471 to joke

garant  151  *v* trere

garce  *f*  473 maid, girl

garçon  *m*  5* miserable, wretched (boy)

garde  *f*  755 watch, surveillance; *loc* metre en g- 30 to entrust; soi prendre
g- 624, 707 to pay attention

garder  *intr*  29, 513, 545 to take care, pay attention; *tr*  193 to keep,
preserve; *refl* 446, 560, 576 to take care, keep watch

garir  *tr*  537 to save, preserve

gas  *m*  8 joke, joking words; *loc* a g- 469 in jest

[gaster]  *tr*  31 to waste

genz  *adj*  108 graceful

gentelise  *f*  412 nobility of character

gentillesce  *f*  192, 210, 362; gentillece 498 nobility of character

gerpir  *tr*  352 to renounce, give up

geu  *m*  105, 948, 958 game; *loc* g- partiz 832* choice, alternative

graine  *f*  279 scarlet vegetable dye

gre  *m*: *loc* de g- 207, 680 freely, on purpose

greignor  *comp adj*  572; greingnor 876*, greater

gris  *m*  96 miniver, squirrel skins

[guenchir] *tr*  268* to turn to the side

[guiler] *intr*  602 to deceive, fool


hart  *f*  816 cord, rope

[haster]  *tr*  638 to hurry, urge

hors  *adv*  439 outside; 535 away; *loc* metre h- 29 to lack

hui  *adv*  18, 320, 556, 714, 718 today; *loc* mes h- 960 from now on

huis  *m*  904 door

hurter  *tr*  810 to dash, hurl; 388 to shake up, surprise; *intr*  640 to ride
    fast, spurring

i  260 = il *pron*
icest  *demon adj*  50 this
iere 53  *imperf 3*, 692, 715 *fut 1*; iert 847 *imperf 3*, 421, 518 *fut 3 of* estre
ilec  *adv*  34 then (on); ilues 787; illec 689 there
ire  *f*  296, 761 anger, rage
ireus  *adj*  84 furious
isneaus  *adj*  109 quick, agile
issi 468 = ici *adv*
issir  *intr*  196, 308*, 463, 535, 678, 746 to leave, go out
issis  *adv*  583 thus, in that way

ja  *adv*  100, 163, 208, 421, 490, 500, 601, 618, 696, 746, 782, 806 never;
        478 ever; 384, 429, 593, 702 already; 684 886, 890 now, at once;
        754, 780 *v* mar; 462, 554, 800 *v* mes
jel = je + le *pron* 781, 783, 817, 859
jengleus  *adj*  831 one who speaks ill
joel  *m*  515 jewel
jons  *m*  517* rushes, reeds
joste  *f*  87 tournament
jou  635; ju 702, 705 = je + le *pron*

lacier  *tr*  817 to fasten, tie with a lace, cord
lait  *m* 11 outrage, offense
lait  *v*  lessier
las  *interj*  166, 184 alas
laz  *m*  176 knot, snare
leece  *f*  587 happiness, joy
lerai 784 *fut 1*; leroie 816 *cond 1 of* lessier *tr*
lessier  *tr*  359, 508, 538 to permit; 593, 784, 834 to leave; 12, 853 to omit;
        36 to release; *refl* 816 to allow oneself; *inf as m* 839 leave-taking,
        leaving
let  *adj*  507 unpleasant, nasty
leu  *m*  72, 286, 694 place, location; *loc* en lieu 122 at the right place
lez  *prep*  717*, 728 next to, near
lié  *adj*  216, 313, 497, 664, 941 happy, joyous
lingnage  *m*  765 ancestry, family
liue  *f*  652 league, measure of distance
[loër]  *tr*  266, 813 to advise, suggest
loge  *f*  292 upper room, gallery

loing *adv: loc* au l- 561 in the end, with time

[loisir] *impers* leüst 102 *pres subj*; loit 15 *pres ind*; lut 119, 574 *pret* to be permitted

lors *adv* 182, 434 then, at that moment

lox *m* 527* praise, honor

lués *adv* 710 immediately


mai *m:lc* avoir bon m- 106 to find pleasure, enjoy oneself

maingne 56 *pres subj 3*; maint 173 *pres ind 3 of* manoir (*q.v.*)

mains *adv* 194, 246, 381, 591, 652, 758, 833, 939 less; *loc* au m- 99, 450 at least; estre du m- to go without saying

maint *adj and pron* 60, 117, 134, 174, 185, 186, 566, 718 many

maintenant *adv* 644 immediately

[mander] *tr* 630 to send for

manel 606* little finger, pinkie

maniere *adj* 544 capable of, apt at

[manoir] *intr* 56, 173, 225 to dwell, abide

mantel *m* 277, 303 cloak, cape

mar *adv* 156 at one's cost, bad luck; *loc* ja m- 754*, 780 ever, for any good result

marche *f* 54*, frontier, border region

maugre *prep: loc* m- mien 799 against my will, despite myself

max *m* 401 pain, torment

[membrer] *impers* 921 remind, cause to come to mind

menuz *adj* 317 fine, finely spread

merci *m* 189, 359, 399 pity; 461 grace; 871, 906 thanks; *loc* la vostre m- 731 please

merveille *f* 297, 609 astonishment, wonder; *loc* venir a m- 557 to astonish

mes *m* 656 messenger

mes *adv* 597, 952 from now on; 513 never; *loc* ainz m- 467; ja m- 462, 554, 800; onques m- 164, 556, 608, 760, 910, 918 never; hui m- 960 *v* hui

mesaamer *tr* 394 to slight, disdain

mesaventure *f* 36 bad luck

[meschoisir] *tr* 880 to miss seeing

mescroire *tr* 597* to mistrust

[mesfaire] *intr* 771 to do wrong

mesprendre *intr* 241, 634, 670, 842 to do wrong, to offend someone

[messeoir] *intr* 697 to displease, offend

mestier *m* 202 need; *loc* estre m- 363 to be necessary

mesure *f* 33 moderation

mi *m* 290, 395, 693 middle

miaus  284  *v* miex

mie  *f*  836* crumb

mie  *adv: loc* ne m- 103, 168, 377, 453, 550, 618, 627, 744, 753, 766, 804, 835, 852, 880, 885, 896, 930, 938 not

miex  20, 26, 49, 242, 438, 738, 887, 929; miez 198; mielz 404; miaus 284 *comp adj* better

mirer  *tr* 343 to look at, contemplate

[moillier]  *tr* 483 to moisten, wet

molt  *adv*  42, 107, 341, 344, 349, 370, 381, 489, 495, 708, 719, 796, 842, 902, 914, 942 much, many; 106, 278, 313, 341, 376, 384, 402, 494, 497, 528, 564, 691, 751, 877, 951 very

mon  *adv* 259 truly, indeed; *loc* m- fere 616, 627 really, truly

monjoie  *f*  224 hill, overlook

mont  *m*  597, 781, 883 world

mont  564  *v*  molt

[monter]  *impers* 229, 586, 764 to concern, have importance

morir  *tr*  512 to kill, cause to die

mostier  *m*  364 church

[mostrer]  *tr*  310, 890 to show

mot  *m: loc*  tot a un m- 884* briefly, at once

movoir  *refl*  212 to start out, leave


na = ne + la  *pron*  858*

nagier  *intr*  46 to navigate (in water)

nel = ne + le *pron* 228, 694, 737

nenil  *neg*  629, 803 no

nercir  *tr*  872 to darken, blacken

noient  *indef pron*  764 nothing; *loc* por n- 629 in vain, uselessly; nient plus 16 no more

nombre  *m: loc*  savoir de n- 962* to know how to count

non  *m*  62, 130, 208, 420, 744, 748, 858, 890, 892 name

[noter]  *tr*  427 to interpret, understand

nu = ne + le *pron* 29, 69, 75, 258, 379, 513, 685, 690, 800, 830, 930

nus  *indef pron*  201, 248, 379, 455, 500, 582, 602; nul 409; nule 135, 463* nobody, no one


o  *prep*  592, 699 with

oel  946  *v*  eulz

oi 760 *pret 1 of* avoir

oïe  *f*  717* ear

oïr  *tr*  62, 74, 259, 467, 548, 718, 729, 759 to hear; *loc*  o- dire 295 hearsay oirre  *m*  660 voyage, journey

oiseus  *adj*  3, 510 idle, useless

ombre  *m or f*  52, 882, 893, 900, 922, 935, 961 reflection

omecide  *m*  541 murderer

on  *indef art*  56 a, one

onques  *adv*  62, 76, 92, 118, 124, 148, 160, 262, 454, 589, 789, 927
    never; *loc* o- mes 164, 556, 608, 760, 910, 918 *v* mes

[oposer]  *tr*  559 to object, reproach

or  *adv*  50, 132, 136, 154, 158, 172, 186, 240, 245, 328, 369, 406, 448,
    468, 484, 506, 594, 603, 616, 620, 626, 630, 640, 716, 722, 724,
    756, 820, 824, 828, 833, 834, 901, 904, 917, 924, 936, 960; ore
    347, 530, 602, 664, 698, 733 now, now then

orains  *adv*  404, 615; orainz 445, 916 just now

oroison  *f*  365 prayer

ostagier  *tr*  523 to retain (by a pledge)

ostel  *m*  81, 418, 713, 746 dwelling, house

ot  59, 63, 64, 73, 88, 106, 116, 126, 127, 297, 304, 315, 549, 609, 675
    *pret 3 of* avoir

ot  74, 729 *pret 3 of* oïr (*q.v.*)

ou = en + le *art*  569, 617, 625, 658, 695, 769, 817, 883, 923

outremer  *m*  504 abroad, across the sea

[outrer]  *tr*  274 to cross, pass through


pais  *f*  127 peace

paliz  *m*  275 post, palissade

panon  *m*  129 feathers on an arrow

par  *adv*  42, 837 *emphatic particle*, very

parfonz  *adj*  880 deep

parlement  *m*  703* conversation

parmi  *prep*  129, 773 through the middle, into

parole  *f*  12, 204, 403, 595, 691, 775, 822, 947* word, speech; *loc* par
    p- 339, 385, 389 orally, by means of words

partir  *refl*  580, 648 to leave; 134 to share (itself); 133 *v* geu

penser  *m*  145, 219, 353, 558, 563, 569, 573, 673, 955 thought

pensis *adj* 216, 584 thoughtful, musing

perron  *m*  287, 811 block of stone, mounting block

[peser]  *impers*  427, 429, 805 to be regrettable, cause pain

petit  *adv: loc* un p- 898 slightly, a little

peüst  18, 81, 308, 728 *imperf subj 3*; peurent 943 *pret 6 of* pouvoir

piece  *f*  698 length, period of time; *loc* pieça 21, 202, 529 long ago, for
    a long time

pieur  *comp adj*  501 worse

pis  *m*  276 chest, breast

[plessier]  *refl*  594 to submit

plet  *m*  819 plea; *loc* bastir p- 146, 464 to make a case (for something)

plume  385  *v*  trere

poi  *adv*  246*, 808 little

poindre  *intr*  641, 649 to ride hard, using spurs

point  *m*  113 moment; 158, 165 situation, state

poise  *v*  peser

pooir  *m*  123, 159, 355, 372, 525, 578, 804 strength, power

por  *prep*  69, 755 despite; p- que 13, 592 in order that; p- ce que 120 because

porpenseement  *adv*  680, 869 deliberately, with thought

pou  *adv*  312, 523 little

praigne  363, 782 *pres subj 3 of* prendre

premerain  *adj*  703 first

preu  *adj*  93*, 110, 315, 417, 528, 891 noble, wise; 839 advantageous; preudome 494, noble; *adv* 726* well, much

preu  *m*  527, 840 profit, advantage

primes  *adv*  408 for the first time

pris  *m*  37 high worth; 380, 758, 902 reputation

[prisier]  *tr*  49, 75 to esteem

prochain  *adj*  543 rapid

proesce  *f*  64, 69 knightly valor

proier  *tr*  188, 511, 826 to beg

pucele  *f*  74, 302, 638 young lady, girl

puet  25, 171, 186, 188, 468, 477, 535, 777, 823, 950, 955 *pres ind 3*; püent 523 *pres ind 6 of* pouvoir

puer  *adv: loc* geter p- 132, 352, 946 to refuse, disdain

puis  *adv*  696, 746, 782, 806, 877, 919 afterward, since

puis  *m*  688, 695, 721, 878, 924, 943 well


q'  *v*  que

qanque  *indef pron*  80, 254, 340, 355, 525; quanque 346 everything

qex 832 = quel *interrog pron*

quant  *conj*  9, 43, 267, 329, 822, 903, 922 since

que  *conj*  16, 26, 33, 39, 90, 114, 135, 159, 164, 240, 321, 341, 346, 357, 361, 393, 440, 494, 573, 739, 753, 786, 819, 910, 956; c' 124, 148, 160, 164, 927 for, because; 220 in order that; 661* before; 75*, 77*, 264 without; 574* with the result that; ne q- 696 if not; que q- 306*, 334, 476 although; 783 if

querre  *tr*  182 to seek; 209, 800, 848 to seek to, to want; *loc* envoyer q- 651 to send for

quit *v* cuidier

ra 37 *pres ind 3 of* re + avoir
rage *f: loc* a grant r- 222 at full speed, in haste
rampone *f* 11 derision, mockery
[reconoistre] *refl: loc* r- a 120-1 to acknowledge oneself to be
[remander] *tr* 655, 657 to send after, recall; *inf as noun* 659 the act of
     sending after
[remanoir] *intr* 958 to remain
[remembrer] *tr* 24 to remind
renc 86 *v* cerchier
rendre *refl* 668 to become a monk, take (religious) orders
reson *f* 267, 289 (good) sense; *loc* r- rendre 340 to answer
retenir *tr* 414, 515* to retain, take into (knightly) service
[retrere] *tr* 236 to mention, call attention to
revengier *refl* 395 to avenge (oneself)
reverdis *adj* 912 revived, exuberant
ridé *adj* 281 pleated
rien *f* 148, 357, 883, 887 person; 383 thing; 100, 228, 443, 609, 853, 952
     anything; *loc* de r- 348, 397 anyhow, in any way; sor toute r- 78
     above all things; n'a r- 819 it is unthinkable
rimer *intr* 46* to steer; to rhyme
roiz *f* 439 net
route *f* 674 escort, party
rubi *m* 139 ruby

[sachier] *tr* 160 to pull; *loc* s- la langue to stick out one's tongue
sairement *m* 838 oath
sajete *f* 128 arrow
sale *f* 287, 678 central hall, room of a castle
samit *m* 303 rich, dyed silk
sans *m* 606 blood
se, s' *conj* 14, 34, 48, 51, 63, 101, 166, 195, 199, 205, 230, 240, 249, 260,
     358, 394, 421, 428, 440, 461, 472, 488, 498, 503, 520, 531, 538,
     540, 555, 594, 632, 635, 684, 687, 690, 700, 705, 730, 740, 742,
     759, 767, 772, 792, 797, 808, 834, 842, 848, 849, 965 if; *loc* se . . .
     non 205, 249, 367, 425, 665, 747, 849, 857 if not
sejor *m* 170 sojourn, act of remaining (some place); *loc* a s- 592 staying
     in one place
sel 327 = si le *pron*; 555 = se le *pron*
semblant *m* 310 expression, appearance; *loc* s- fere 432, 596 to give the
     impression, reveal an attitude

sen  *m*  572, 876 wise, sensible action

seneschaus  *m*  290 seneschal, head steward of a household

sens  *m*  3, 6, 35, 39, 140, 376, 425, 867, 914, 956 intelligence, understanding; 426 meaning; 193 sanity; *loc*  en son s- sane

sens  *poss pron*  375 his

seoir 227, 327, 721; seïr 728  *intr*  to be situated, to sit

set 136, 339, 448, 479, 486, 582 *pres ind 3*; seüsse 475 *perf subj 1*; seüssiez
*perf subj 5*; seüst 395 *perf subj 3 of* savoir

seue  *poss adj*  857 her

seur  *prep*  317, 878 on, over

seurcot  *m*  278 overgarment (for men and women)

seürs  *adj*  253 certain, sure

seürté  *f*  791 confidence, trust

seus  *adj*  162 alone

si  *poss adj*  322, 330, 581, 712 his

si  *adv*  253, 365, 381, 747 thus; *loc*  s- fait, ferez  *v*  fere; *conj* 67, 122, 198,
266, 356, 427, 456, 479, 511, 521, 571, 585, 600, 605, 633, 689,
736, 737, 784, 813, 870, 880, 894 and, and also; 110, 619, 905 even
though, however; de s- que 127 until; par s- que 252* on the condition that; s- que 482 so that, with the result that; s- comme 642, 711
just as

siecle  *m*  502 world, age, era

sifet  *adj*  370* such

simplece  *f*  540 goodness, virtue

sire  *adj*  255, 796 proud, masterful

sofime  *m*  257 false, deceitful argument

sofrete  *f*  203 deprivation, misery

[sofrir]  *tr*  195, 508; *refl* 392 to allow, permit; *intr* 511 to refrain

soing  *m: loc*  estre en s- 562 to be concerned, worried

solaz  *m*  175 pleasure

some  *f: loc*  ce est la s- 409 in short

son  *m: loc*  dusqu'en s- 647; jusqu'en s- 850 to the limit, the utmost

sot  72, 86, 104 *pret 3 of* savoir

soupeçon  *f*  666 uneasiness, doubt

souploïer  *intr*  40* to bow

soutise  *adj*  623* intelligent, observant

[sozrire]  *intr*  244, 874 to smile

suen  *poss adj*  65 his


tantost  *adv*  299 just before

tant  *adv*  152, 566 so many, so much; *conj* de t- que, com 312, 614 as
much as; de t- comme, que 738, 943, however much; de t- 738 as

much; t- que 224, 273 until; t- comme 357, 674 as much as; *m pl* 97 times (*count word*)

tanz *v* tant

teche *f* 59 quality, characteristic; 539 bad quality, evil action

tençon *f* 271 dispute, argument

[tendre] *tr: loc* mener t- 392 to hold back, keep on tight reins

tenir *intr* 501, 528, 550, 632, 702, 737, 754, 770, 830; *refl* 411, 654 to consider as; *loc* soi en t- a 265 to agree about something; t- chier 172 to cherish

tens *m* 458; tans 106 time; *loc* en t- 122 in time, at the right time

tente *v* tant

tex 56 *m sg of* tel *indef pron*

tiers *m* 126 a third; *loc* soi t- 213 oneself as the third, with two others

toise *f* 316, 879 length measure, six feet

tor *m* 829 way out (of a situation)

torner *tr* 277 to turn; *loc* t- son afere 88, 460 to turn one's attention, interest; 42, 761 to turn into, turn out as

tost *adv* 28, 31, 37, 593, 640, 691, 761, 889 quickly, soon

tot *adj and indef pron* 98, 111, 137, 240, 245, 434, 553, 597, 707, 757, 855, 932; toz 345, 375, 545, 606 all; tot *adv* 536, 745, 868, 869, 889; toz 524, 579, 912 completely

trace *f: loc* en la t- 726* in the right direction

[travailler] *tr* 558 to torment

[trecier] *tr* 299* to plait hair

trere *tr* 570 to pull, draw; 128 to shoot (an arrow); *loc* t- a garant 150 to call as witness; parmi l'ueil la plume t- 385* to fool, deceive

tres *prep* 408 since; *adv: loc* t- parmi 773 completely in the middle, straight into

trespasser *tr* 263*, 323 pass by (without acknowledging), ignore

trespenser *intr* 324 to become thoughtful

trestote *adv* 611 completely

treü *m* 115 tribute, duty

tuit *indef pron* 67 all


ueil *m* 385 eye

un *num: loc* un et un 23 one after the other

user *tr* 2 to use; 31 to exhaust


vallet *m* 215, 288*, 637 squire

vanche *f* 282 periwinkle

veer *tr* 421, 925 to refuse

veez 227; vez 892, 901 *imper 5 of* veoir *tr*

veil   1, 2, 4, 266, 361, 411, 526, 752, 824 *pres ind 1;* velt 114, 154, 548,
   635, 685, 690, 896 *pres ind 3;* veille 667 *pres subj 3 of* voloir
venir   *tr*  450 to become; *intr: loc*  v- mieus 20, 242, 438 to be preferable;
   *m* 388, 405 arrival
ver   *m*  96 fur of two shades
vermaus   *adj*  283, 480; vermeulz 482; vermeille 296, 298, 610 scarlet, red
verté   *f*  151 truth; *loc*  a v- 344 as a witness; par v- 387 in truth, truly
veüe   *f*  150 eyesight
vez   *v*  veez
vilains   *m*  160 peasant; *adj* 8 coarse, vulgar
vilenie   *f*  533, 806; vilanie 699 coarse, non-courtly behavior, action
vis   *m; loc*  il miest v- 814 it seems to me
vis   *m*  141, 349, 483, 522, 540 face
voil   39, 753, 767, 770, 842 *pres ind 1;* volt 306 *pres ind 3;* voilliez 798
   *pres subj 5;* vorroie 250 *cond 1;* vosist 80, 90, 101, 598 *imperf subj 3;*
   vousist 410 *imperf subj 3 of* voloir
voir   *m*  truth; *loc*  v- dire 25, 322, 371, 628 to tell the truth; *adv* 391,
   768, 801, 803 truly, really
voiseuse   *adj*  567 sly, clever
voist   643   *pres subj 3 of* aler
voloir   *m*  328 desire, wish
vuel   *m; loc*  son v- 163 if he had his way

LI'